THE MINDFUL ART OF SWEDISH DEATH CLEANING

A GENTLE SCANDINAVIAN METHOD TO DECLUTTER, DOWNSIZE, ORGANIZE, AND LEAVE A LOVING LEGACY

LINNEA M. BERGMAN

© **Copyright 2025 by The Emerald Society - All rights reserved.**

The content contained within this book may not be reproduced, duplicated, or transmitted without direct written permission from the author or the publisher.

Under no circumstances will any blame or legal responsibility be held against the publisher, or author, for any damages, reparation, or monetary loss due to the information contained within this book, either directly or indirectly.

Legal Notice:

This book is copyright protected. It is only for personal use. You cannot amend, distribute, sell, use, quote or paraphrase any part, or the content within this book, without the consent of the author or publisher.

Disclaimer Notice:

Please note that the information contained within this document is for educational and entertainment purposes only. All effort has been executed to present accurate, up-to-date, and reliable, complete information. No warranties of any kind are declared or implied. Readers acknowledge that the author is not engaging in the rendering of legal, financial, medical, or professional advice. The content within this book has been derived from various sources. Please consult a licensed professional before attempting any techniques outlined in this book.

By reading this document, the reader agrees that under no circumstances is the author responsible for any losses, direct or indirect, which are incurred as a result of the use of the information contained within this document, including but not limited to errors, omissions, or inaccuracies.

A SPECIAL GIFT TO MY READERS

Visit emeraldsocpublishing.com to download your FREE copy!

LEAVE A REVIEW

Don't forget to share the love and **leave your <u>Amazon review</u>** for:

CONTENTS

Disclaimer	ix
BOOK I	1
Ode to the Clutter We Once Loved	3
Confessions from the Attic	5
Embracing the Swedish Death Cleaning Mindset	9
The Gift of Letting Go: Freeing Yourself and Your Family	18
BOOK II	23
Start Small, Start Now	25
The Room-by-Room Swedish Method	40
Donation, Disposal, and Doing Good	59
BOOK III	74
Preserving What Matters	76
Family, Friends, and Tricky Conversations	88
The Emotional Terrain of Letting Go	102
Sustaining Simplicity	118
The Gentle Art of Beginning Again	131
BONUS: Swedish Death Cleaning Toolkit	133
Postscript	145
Join Our Tribe	147
Bibliography	149

DISCLAIMER

Dearest Reader,

Despite its ominous name, *Swedish Death Cleaning* will not hasten your demise.

It may, however, lead to the following side effects:

- Mild smugness from finally finding your dining table under the mail pile.
- Unexpected laughter while holding an object you once thought you'd definitely need someday.
- Frequent coffee breaks disguised as "emotional processing time."

This book also references *fika* approximately 83 times. You'll soon understand why; it's basically therapy, but with pastries.

If at any point you find yourself overwhelmed, stop immediately and apply caffeine, sugar, or humor as needed.

BOOK I

The Philosophy:

A Gentle Swedish Approach to Life and Legacy

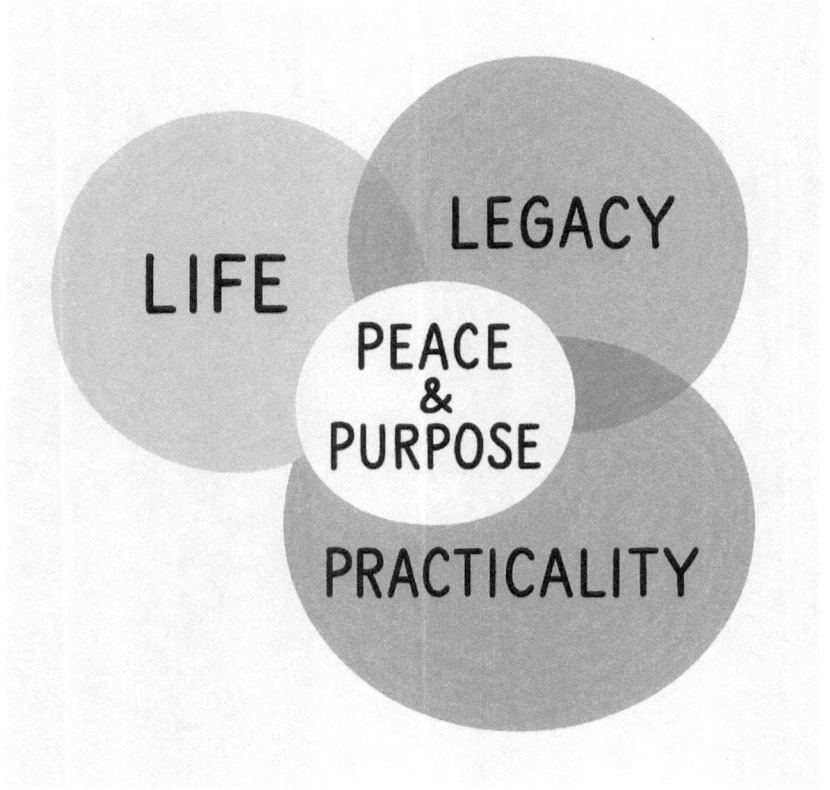

ODE TO THE CLUTTER WE ONCE LOVED

I swore I'd clean the attic years ago,
But somehow found three blenders in a row.
The scarves, the shoes, the random bits of string,
My house could host its own museum wing.

I've kept each mug from every friend I've known,
And fifty jars, "for plants I'll someday grow."
My junk drawer laughs, its chaos knows no bounds,
A shrine to batteries that can't be found.

The photo box explodes, my youth, my hair!
(Who was that girl with hope and zero care?)
I hold each relic, smiling through the sigh,
And whisper, "Time to let you go. Goodbye."

But first, fika. Coffee cures all fear.
A pastry, please, for bravery sincere.
For life's too short to drown in dust and stuff,
I've hoarded love; that's quite enough.

So here's to letting go with grace and flair,
To leaving space for joy and fresher air,
To laughter, light, and peace that softly gleams,
Our death cleaning's the start of sweeter dreams.

CONFESSIONS FROM THE ATTIC

I'd like to start with a confession: I once found four fondue sets in my attic. Four. I cannot remember ever hosting a fondue party, nor do I know why one human being would need *four*. Yet there they were, stacked beside a box of old scarves and piles of children's artwork that even my children, now adults, couldn't identify. I stood in that attic, surrounded by memories, dust bunnies, and a growing sense of dread. How did all this stuff come to be? And, more importantly, why did it feel so hard to let any of it go?

If you're a woman over fifty, chances are you know this feeling all too well. Your house isn't just a house; it's a museum of treasures, a warehouse of just-in-case items, and a retirement home for every gadget you swore would change your life (hello ab roller, Zumba DVDs, and that dusty set of resistance bands still in the packaging). Add in the gifts you never quite loved, the heirlooms you inherited but don't know what to do with, and suddenly you're the proud owner of Mount Overwhelm. You hesitate to toss things because the second you do, you'll probably need it. Cue the guilt trip for even thinking about rehoming family memorabilia.

But perhaps, through all clutter, the heaviest burden is that quiet little fear whispering that someday, someone you love will have to sort through it all.

I truly believe that women deserve homes that feel peaceful, not stressful. You deserve to wake up each day knowing your space reflects who you are now, not just who you were at twenty, or what someone else passed down to you. And the truth is, clutter isn't just taking up square footage, it's taking up *headspace*. A tidy, intentional home brings calm, clarity, and a sense of control that spills into every corner of your life. I want to help you free yourself from the hidden burdens of stuff so you can breathe easier, enjoy your days, and leave a deeply loving, thoughtful legacy, all without guilt, drama, or the nightmare of a dumpster rental.

This is where Swedish death cleaning comes in. Don't let the name scare you. In Sweden, it's called döstädning (yes, it sounds serious, but trust me, it isn't). It means "death cleaning" in the literal sense, but in reality, it's about thoughtfully going through your belongings and letting go of what you no longer need, so your loved ones won't have to do it for you. It's a tradition rooted in care, kindness, and a little bit of Scandinavian practicality. And, as I've discovered, it doesn't have to be sad or scary. In fact, it can be a surprisingly joyful, even funny, process (sometimes involving fondue sets).

Why focus on women over fifty? Because we're at a unique crossroads. Many of us are caring for both children and aging parents. Some of us are downsizing or thinking about retirement. We are the keepers of family stories and the stewards of family stuff. We know what it means to want to pass on something meaningful, not just boxes of things to sort. I've seen friends struggle to clear out their parents' homes, feeling both love and resentment as they sift through decades of belongings. I've also seen women step into this process for themselves and discover relief, pride, and even laughter along the way.

So, here's what you can expect from this book: a mix of practical steps and heartfelt wisdom. I'll walk you through how to start, what questions to ask, and when to call in reinforcements (or at least a friend with strong opinions about knick-knacks). You'll find checklists, worksheets, and stories from other women who have been right where you are. I'll share rituals and small ceremonies for letting go, because sometimes a proper goodbye is what we need most. You'll find suggestions for tricky conversations with family, ways to honor your memories, and even tips for the "what if I need it" items.

Remember that there's no one-size-fits-all here. This is not a cold, clinical approach, nor is it a generic decluttering manual. You won't find me telling you to toss everything but your favorite mug and a single pair of socks. Nor will you need to become a minimalist monk. I understand the urge to keep your grandmother's teacups, even if you only drink coffee. I know the sting of letting go of your child's first school project, and the relief of finally donating the treadmill you swore you'd use.

And most importantly, I want you to know that every emotion you feel along the way is normal. Guilt, nostalgia, overwhelm, even joy—they all belong. This book is a gentle, judgment-free companion. You set the pace. You make the decisions. I'll be here with stories, suggestions, and the occasional nudge when you need it.

Let's be clear: this is not about perfection. It's about creating space for what matters most, for you and those you love. It's about finding clarity in your surroundings, and peace in your heart. It's about laughing at your own collection of fondue sets and choosing, just maybe, to keep the one that brings you a smile.

So, are you ready? Not for a drastic purge, not for a marathon cleaning session, but for a thoughtful, meaningful journey. One box, one memory, one conversation at a time. I invite you to take the first small step with me. Let's make your home not just a storage space, but a place that truly supports your life today and the legacy you want to leave tomorrow.

   Welcome. Let's begin.

EMBRACING THE SWEDISH DEATH CLEANING MINDSET

There's a moment I'll never forget.

My friend Jen rang me up, torn between laughing and cringing. Her teenage daughter had stumbled across a book on her nightstand titled *Swedish Death Cleaning* and immediately asked, "Mom... are you planning your funeral?" For the record, Jen wasn't writing a eulogy; she was knee-deep in reorganizing her linen closet.

That little mix-up captures the biggest misconception about Swedish death cleaning. The name makes it sound like something you do at the very end, a grim checklist to prep for your final curtain call. In reality? It's the opposite. As Jen quickly discovered (and as you'll see in these pages) Swedish death cleaning is not morbid at all. It's about decluttering with purpose, making room for what matters, and yes, laughing at yourself when you wonder why you've been storing three generations' worth of bath towels. This process is less about death and more about life: reclaiming your space, your energy, and maybe even your sense of humor along the way.

Döstädning: Swedish Wisdom for Real Life

Döstädning, in its most straightforward translation, means "death cleaning," where "dö" is death and "städning" is cleaning. But before you picture yourself organizing your belongings with one foot in the grave, it's worth pausing to really understand the Swedish intent.

Döstädning is not about dark thoughts or planning for your last days, but living more intentionally, with a clear eye on what you truly need and what you wish to leave behind. The philosophy goes far beyond the act of sorting. In Sweden, döstädning is a practical, thoughtful approach to life's accumulation. It's an ongoing conversation with oneself about what to keep, what to pass on, and what stories each item carries. It's a recognition that our homes don't just hold things; they hold meaning, history, and sometimes a little too much chaos.

Compared to other decluttering crazes, döstädning stands apart in both spirit and execution. While Marie Kondo asks you to touch each object and ask if it "sparks joy," döstädning invites you to consider legacy. It asks, "Will this matter to someone after I'm gone?" or simply, "Does this still serve me?"

The Swedish method is less about achieving a minimalist aesthetic or displaying perfectly folded socks. Instead, it's driven by practicality and emotional clarity. There's no pressure to get rid of everything or to live with bare walls and empty shelves. The focus is on thoughtful curation: choosing with purpose and honesty, not out of guilt or trendiness. Where other approaches can feel rigid or even performative, döstädning gives you permission to honor the sentimental while also releasing the unnecessary.

EMBRACING THE SWEDISH DEATH CLEANING MINDSET

Swedes have a reputation for sensible living, and this tradition runs deep. I once spent time with a Swedish family during their annual döstädning ritual, which unfolded not as a frantic purge but as a gentle, almost celebratory review of their home's contents. They gathered in the living room with coffee and cinnamon buns (fika is mandatory), each person bringing items they'd found while tidying: an old winter coat, a stack of postcards from relatives, mismatched candlesticks. The conversation was open and honest: Who could use this coat? Does anyone want these postcards? Sometimes an object sparked laughter; sometimes it brought a story. The family made collective decisions about donating, keeping, or discarding, but never rushed or shamed anyone into a choice. One daughter decided to keep her father's chess set, even though she hadn't played in years; it reminded her of long evenings together at the kitchen table. Her brother let go of a collection of broken Lego sets. But truly, what struck me most was the absence of judgment and urgency, just a steady commitment to lightening the load, together.

Central to döstädning's appeal is its flexibility. There is no checklist that fits every home or every person. Some may start in the garage, others with photo albums or kitchen drawers. You choose your own pace (bit by bit or in weekend bursts) depending on your energy and emotional bandwidth. The categories you tackle and what you decide to keep are entirely up to you. Someone might find it easy to part with old clothes, but impossible to let go of their children's artwork; another may feel the opposite. Swedes embrace this personal variation without apology. They recognize that every life contains unique threads of memory and attachment, so each person's process will look different.

Furthermore, what makes döstädning so adaptable is its focus on communication with yourself and with your loved ones. You're encouraged to talk about your decisions, share stories behind objects, and ask for help when needed. There are no rigid rules;

only guiding principles rooted in kindness and awareness. If a certain item brings comfort or pride, keep it without shame. If it weighs you down or has lost its meaning, give yourself permission to let it go. This creates room for new experiences, and for those who come after you to understand not just what you kept, but why.

Unlike trends that push for radical minimalism or tidy perfection, döstädning honors the complexity of our lives. It allows for nostalgia while making space for clarity. It celebrates both practicality and sentimentality, sometimes in the same shoebox. Through this uniquely Swedish lens, cleaning becomes an act of care, reflection, and quiet transformation.

To-Do: Heritage Notes

As you move through this process, consider keeping *Heritage Notes*. Nothing fancy, just a notebook or worksheet where you jot down what you're keeping and, more importantly, why. Add the story behind a photo, or note who you hope will love that necklace as much as you did. Ask yourself:

What does this mean to me?

Who should have this?

Here's the magic part: sharing these stories turns everyday items into connections across generations. When families gather to sort through belongings, the conversation usually drifts into laughter, "Remember when...?" stories, and the kind of memories no storage bin could ever hold. Because at the end of the day, your true legacy isn't the stuff; it's the stories, the meaning, and the love you attach to them.

EMBRACING THE SWEDISH DEATH CLEANING MINDSET

Why We Are the Perfect Pioneers

If you have ever been the person who knows where to find the missing puzzle piece, remembers every family birthday, and can whip up your grandmother's cornbread recipe from memory, you already know the strength and skill that comes with experience. We are more than just keepers of calendars and casserole dishes; we're the glue that holds together stories, traditions, and sometimes an entire household's worth of oddities. More than age, this is about perspective. With years comes a keen sense of what carries real value: what is worth holding close, what can be set free, and what makes a house feel like home. You've lived enough seasons to see trends come and go, watched loved ones grow up and move on, and you understand the bittersweet beauty of change.

Often, we find ourselves not only managing our own lives but acting as the family's unofficial historian. You might be the one who stores the photo albums from five decades, the holiday ornaments that have survived twelve moves, and your grown children's first report cards (let's face it, nobody else will remember whose handwriting is on those faded labels). Passing down a quilt stitched by your mother or sharing a handwritten recipe card with a grandchild is offering a piece of your own narrative. Women are the ones who remember Uncle Lou's story behind that chipped mug, or which Christmas the turquoise tinsel first made its appearance. If there is a family tradition to carry on or an heirloom to protect, it most likely lands in your capable hands.

Yet this role comes with its own set of challenges. Many of us are what experts call the "sandwich generation," balancing care for aging parents while also supporting adult children (sometimes even grandchildren). You might be fielding requests for help with a parent's downsizing one week, then negotiating storage space for your daughter's college textbooks the next. It's a juggling act that requires patience, resilience, and often a strong cup of coffee. The pressure to preserve memories for everyone, to act as both archivist and caretaker, can feel overwhelming at times. The emotional toll of sorting through a parent's belongings after their passing or deciding what to do with childhood mementos is real and deserves compassion.

But here's the good news: women over fifty are uniquely qualified for this work, not because it is easy but because we possess a rare combination of wisdom, humor, and discernment. We know how to prioritize. We appreciate nostalgia but can weigh it against practicality. We understand that true legacy isn't measured in boxes but in the laughter around the dinner table or the comfort in a favorite old scarf. If you choose to approach Swedish death cleaning as an act of intention rather than obligation, you will reclaim power over your space and your legacy. You will set a tone for your family that says, "We honor our memories, but we don't drown in them."

Taking action in this way models empowerment and self-respect. When you sort through belongings with purpose, you send a message to everyone around you (family, friends, even neighbors) that it's possible to honor the past without giving up control of the present. This mindset is contagious. One woman I know inspired not only her sisters but her own children to begin their own form of death cleaning, not out of fear or pressure, but because they saw how much lighter and more joyful she felt afterwards.

So, if you've ever felt like the only adult in the room, here's your chance to finally turn that superpower into something that actually serves *you*, and the people you love most. You don't have to tackle everything in one heroic weekend, and perfection is not on the checklist. Every drawer cleared, every story passed down, is an act of wisdom and love. This isn't just decluttering; you will be rewriting the script to show that true legacy isn't measured in the stuff we leave behind, but in the peace, guidance, and sense of purpose we pass forward.

From Overwhelm to Action

Standing at the entrance to a cluttered attic or staring down that hallway closet, you might find your heart beating a little faster, palms growing clammy. The sheer volume of boxes, bins, and baskets (each one threatening to burst with forgotten odds and ends) can stop even the bravest woman in her tracks.

I've been there myself, frozen by the mountain of holiday decorations teetering on a shelf, the mysterious "miscellaneous" bins, the stacks of yellowing magazines someone was supposed to read in 2004. The longer you look, the more these things seem to multiply. It's as though your possessions have formed a tiny, chaotic army determined to defend their right to remain undisturbed. You try to start, maybe with a single shoebox, but the moment you pull out a tangle of old ballet slippers or a collection of mismatched Tupperware lids, you feel the urge to back away slowly. This is analysis paralysis at its finest: too many decisions, too many emotions, and suddenly you're exhausted before you've even begun.

The first thing I want you to know is that this overwhelm is completely normal. There's no secret club where everyone else knows how to breeze through decades of stuff without batting an eyelash. The fear of starting is real, as the "what if I make a mistake?" or "what if I get rid of something important?" soundtrack plays on repeat in our minds. You may worry about stirring up old memories or facing decisions that feel heavier than they should. It's tempting to believe the only way forward is to tackle everything at once, but that's a myth. You don't need to transform your house in a frantic weekend spree or channel your inner superhero. In fact, I give you full permission to take the tiniest step possible: one drawer, one shelf, or just one single item. If all you do today is toss out those expired coupons in your purse, that's progress. And progress, not perfection, is what we're after.

When the job feels too big, it helps to break it into bite-sized pieces. One tool I love is what I call the Clutter Hotspot Map. This isn't a fancy diagram or something that needs graph paper; just grab a notebook and walk through your home with open eyes. Make a simple list of the areas that attract the most clutter or cause you the most stress. For me, it was always the hall closet (where coats went to disappear) and a kitchen junk drawer that seemed bottomless. Write down each hotspot as you spot it: attic, linen cupboard, bedside table, garage shelves. Don't judge or overthink, just record what you see. Once you have your map, pick one location, preferably the smallest or least emotional to start. Set a timer for ten minutes and do what you can in that window. Ten minutes is enough time for a quick win, but short enough to keep dread at bay.

This approach may sound simple, but it certainly is powerful. Momentum builds with each small victory. The pride you feel after clearing one shelf will fuel you for the next. Celebrate those wins! Don't wait for an Instagram-worthy "after" photo or an empty garage before you pat yourself on the back. Drop off one bag at Goodwill and treat yourself to coffee afterward. Recycle that stack of old catalogs and enjoy the satisfaction of seeing space open up on your counter.

One woman I worked with, Denise, struggled for years with her overflowing basement. The idea of cleaning it out completely overwhelmed her, so she set herself a tiny challenge: ten minutes a day, every day after dinner. Sometimes she filled a bag for donation; sometimes she just sorted through old photos or untangled a box of cords no one could identify anymore. The magic wasn't in doing everything at once, but in showing up for herself day after day, even when she didn't feel like it. After two months, her basement had space for an actual yoga mat (imagine that!). More importantly, Denise realized she didn't have to dread her stuff anymore; she could face it in manageable doses and feel lighter with every session.

Your First Step

Take five minutes now. Walk through your house with your favorite pen and list every area that makes you sigh or groan when you pass by (no need for shame here). Maybe it's under the bathroom sink or that mysterious bin in the laundry room marked "random." There's no wrong answer. When you're finished, circle just one spot (the easiest one if you want) and commit to spending just ten minutes there tomorrow.

Remind yourself: action conquers paralysis, one small step at a time.

THE GIFT OF LETTING GO: FREEING YOURSELF AND YOUR FAMILY

There's a certain tenderness in deciding to let something go, especially when it has lived with you for years or even decades. Yet, true generosity sometimes means releasing your grip—on boxes, on expectations, on guilt. Swedish death cleaning, at its heart, is one of the greatest gifts you can give both yourself and the people you cherish most. It's an act of love far more than a task on your to-do list. Doing this work now spares your family from difficult decisions later, and offers you a kind of peace that can turn down the constant hum of anxiety in your mind. Imagine for a moment the quiet after the clutter is gone. No one else will have to wonder if those old letters are precious family artifacts or just bills from the 1980s. You get to decide what holds value, which stories remain, and what finally gets released without second-guessing.

Sleeping better is not just a cliché here. One reader told me she hadn't realized how much her clutter was weighing on her until she cleared her bedroom of old boxes. She described waking up rested, no longer staring at those stacks every morning, no longer feeling like unfinished business was looming over her head. Letting go of things is not always easy, but it can be surprisingly liberating.

Legacy isn't measured by how much you can stockpile in your garage or how tightly you can cling to things "just in case." It's about thoughtfully curating what actually matters so the people you love are left with a clear sense of who you were, rather than a confusing scavenger hunt through decades of forgotten knickknacks.

Think about it: do you want your kids to remember your grandmother's laugh, her strength, and her story… or just that chipped gravy boat that nobody's used since 1987? Do you want them to feel warmth and connection when they look around, or to feel like they're drowning in a sea of mismatched Tupperware, dusty photo albums, and boxes labeled "miscellaneous" (a.k.a. the Bermuda Triangle of storage)?

And there's a freedom in this process that extends well beyond clearing space on a shelf. You'll notice cleaning becomes easier; fewer things mean less dusting, less sorting, fewer "where did I put that?" moments. You'll rediscover forgotten corners in your home, maybe even spots that invite a favorite chair or a vase of fresh flowers. As your surroundings grow simpler, your mind will feel clearer, too. You will start to see what you truly value: perhaps handwritten recipes from a friend, a single photograph that always makes you smile, or the necklace you wear every holiday.

To make the immediate benefits tangible and real, here's a quick scan of what you'll likely feel as you begin letting go:

- More space in your home. You might even find room for hobbies you've been putting off (hello, painting table!).
- Easier cleaning and organizing. Fewer objects mean less time spent searching and tidying.

- Sharper clarity about what matters most. When only the meaningful remains, decision-making feels easier and your priorities become obvious.
- A lighter heart and less guilt. You stop carrying responsibility for items that no longer serve you.
- Less anxiety about "what happens if..." scenarios. You know your loved ones won't be left guessing about your wishes or drowning in your past.

That's the gift of Swedish death cleaning. Swap loss for clarity. Make sure the story your loved ones inherit is one of intention, meaning, and love, not obligation and guilt. Shape a legacy that speaks louder than any object ever could.

Reframing Your Legacy with Stories, Not Stuff

I have noticed that the most meaningful legacies rarely come from the objects themselves but from the memories that cling to them. The laughter at a family dinner, the stories whispered over an old photograph, the warmth in a worn quilt passed down with a tale attached. When you pause to ask, "What story does this cherished item tell, and who would appreciate hearing it?" you begin to shift focus from physical things to living history. A chipped teacup may not fetch much at an estate sale, but if it's the one your mother used every Sunday, it carries a universe of love. Passing down these stories, not just the items, is what creates connection. Imagine taking a moment to write a short note and tuck it into a recipe box before giving it to your daughter: "This is the spice cake your grandmother baked every Christmas. She always said the secret was extra nutmeg and a dash of laughter." Suddenly, what was once just a box becomes a bridge between generations.

Sharing stories in this way invites your loved ones to value what mattered most to you, and even find comfort and delight in objects they might otherwise overlook. I've sat at many family tables where a battered rolling pin or faded apron sparked lively conversation, laughter, and sometimes even tears. One of my favorite gatherings happened when relatives came together for what was supposed to be sorting out "stuff." Instead, we spent hours telling stories about each object: how my uncle once tried (and failed) to bake bread with that rolling pin, how my aunt wore that brooch to every graduation. The real treasures emerged from our shared memories. The objects became anchors for stories, and suddenly, even the youngest children listened intently as we relived moments they'd never witnessed but now would never forget.

To help you focus on what truly matters as you sort through your home, I encourage you to create a simple worksheet or notebook where you jot down not just what you're keeping, but why. This exercise doesn't need to be complicated or time-consuming. For each item you want to save or pass along, answer a few questions: "Why did I keep this? What memory does it hold? Who should receive it?" You might add details like where the item came from or the story behind its significance. This practice can be surprisingly liberating; it allows you to be intentional and thoughtful without feeling pressure to keep everything out of guilt or habit. It also gives your loved ones context, so they know why that particular vase mattered or who wore that silk scarf on her wedding day.

If you're unsure where to start, try these worksheet prompts:

- Describe the item.
- What memory or story is attached to it?
- Who do you think would appreciate this most?

- Is there a special occasion or tradition linked to it?
- Why do you want this passed on or kept?

Writing these notes will help you clarify your own attachments and make peace with letting go of what no longer serves you. Remember: less stuff means more focus on the heirlooms and moments that define your life's story. When your home holds fewer items but each one is rich in story and meaning, your environment feels lighter and more intentional.

Legacy isn't static; it evolves as new stories are born and new memories created. The gifts you leave behind aren't limited to possessions; they live on in laughter at family gatherings, in recipes prepared on holidays, in letters tucked inside old books waiting to be discovered by curious grandchildren. Your story lives on not in closets but in hearts, woven through the lives of those who come after you.

As you reflect on what legacy means to you, remember: every story shared is a gift more lasting than any object could ever be. This is how we turn letting go into an act of deep love and enduring connection: one memory, one note, one story at a time.

BOOK II

THE MINDFUL ART OF SWEDISH DEATH CLEANING

The Practice:

Step-by-Step Decluttering for Women

START SMALL, START NOW

The One-Drawer Miracle: Your Starter Project

Think of this as the pilot episode of your decluttering journey. This is the one that proves you've got what it takes before the big drama begins. You know how in those crime shows, one tiny clue cracks open the whole case? I wish my kitchen junk drawer held the secret to who keeps mixing rubber bands with birthday candles, but alas, no such luck. What it does hold, however, is the perfect place to start.

Here's the deal: Swedish death cleaning doesn't begin in the basement, attic, or that closet you've been side-eyeing since 2003. It begins with something manageable. One drawer. That's it. Not the one stuffed with your kids' preschool art or your grandmother's recipe cards (save the sentimental landmines for later). Pick a drawer that feels neutral. Everyday. Boring.

Why? Because success loves momentum. Tackling one small space gives you an easy win, and that win becomes the proof you need: you *can* do this. You'll see instant progress, feel a tiny rush of accomplishment, and maybe even start to believe that clearing a lifetime of clutter is possible. The One-Drawer Miracle isn't about the drawer, it's about you. It's a little vote of confidence that says, "If I can handle this, I can handle the next thing, too."

So, pick a drawer you use often but don't have strong feelings about. Kitchen junk drawers are classics; I once found a key from the '90s and enough paperclips for a store. Nightstands are another good choice, as they attract stray glasses, expired medicine, and forgotten knickknacks. The bathroom vanity drawer works well, too: clear out old makeup, dried floss, tired hair ties. The main thing is to avoid starting with anything sentimental, like family jewelry or baby clothes. Just keep it easy and start building momentum.

Before dumping the drawer out, gather a trash bag for broken pens or trash, a donation box for duplicates or unused items, and a cleaning cloth. It may seem like overkill for a small drawer, but setting yourself up means you won't wander off looking for supplies. As you empty the drawer, sort items into clear categories: keep, toss, donate, or relocate. If something, like a screwdriver, belongs elsewhere, set it aside to move later. Handle each object and ask:

- *Do I use this?*
- *Does it serve me now?*
- *Am I keeping it "just in case" or out of habit?*

As a foundation of decluttering, it is recommended to **toss duplicates** and **discard anything broken or expired**. Let go of bent measuring spoons and mysterious keys. Only keep items that truly earn their spot (no freeloaders!). And, please, don't overthink this process. This isn't your wedding album; it's batteries, receipts, and maybe a stray birthday candle.

When the drawer is empty, take a breath and enjoy the clean

slate. Wipe it thoroughly to refresh your space and mindset. Only return the useful, needed items, grouping them by function if possible. Drawer dividers or old checkbook boxes can help, but don't worry about perfection; progress matters more right now.

I can guarantee you'll notice a psychological boost right away. Research shows that even small visible improvements create motivation. The next morning, when you see a tidy, organized drawer, you might gain a bit of control and confidence. Suddenly, sorting the linen closet won't seem insurmountable. Each little win generates momentum for tackling bigger spaces.

One-Drawer Miracle Checklist

- Choose a low-emotion drawer (kitchen junk, nightstand, bathroom vanity).
- Gather: trash bag, donation box, cleaning cloth.
- Empty contents onto a table or counter.
- Sort into: keep, toss, donate, relocate.
- Wipe drawer interior thoroughly.
- Return only what truly belongs; organize as you go.

One-Drawer Miracle Checklist

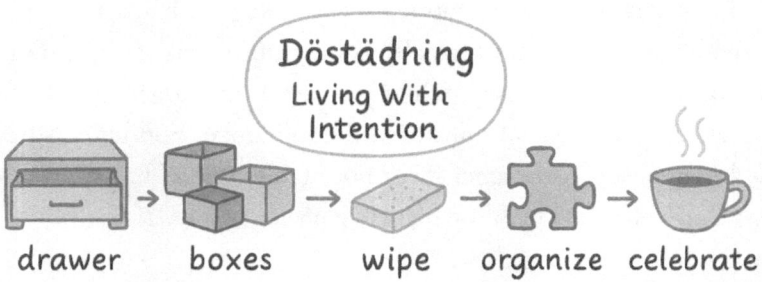

I will say this again (and again!): celebrate your victories, no matter how tiny they seem. Take a moment to appreciate your accomplishment. Snap a photo of your gloriously organized drawer or text it to a friend who gets it. (Pro tip: don't send it to your sister-in-law who color-codes her sock drawer; you don't need that kind of energy right now.) The point is to acknowledge the satisfaction of carving out a little island of order in the sea of chaos.

Because as you build confidence, one drawer will turn into two. Two drawers will lead to a closet. Before you know it, the mountain of stuff that once felt overwhelming will start to look like a series of small, manageable hills. And that shift? That's the real miracle.

Where to Begin in Your Home

Every home has its own geography of chaos. Somehow, certain areas attract clutter like a magnet. Maybe it's the entryway table, buried beneath keys, mail, and the odd reusable bag. Perhaps it's the laundry room shelf, teetering with orphan socks and half-used detergents. Even a garage shelf or the basket next to your favorite chair can morph into a miniature landfill if left unchecked. These are your clutter hotspots, the ones that seem to collect random objects without your permission and manage to raise your blood pressure on sight. A hotspot isn't always the largest mess in the house; it's the place that makes you sigh, grumble, or mutter something unprintable every time you pass by.

It helps to see these trouble zones mapped out visually. Drawing a simple sketch of your home or printing a template lets you pinpoint exactly where the clutter loves to gather. Don't worry if your map looks more like a kindergarten drawing than an architect's blueprint. The point is to identify, not impress. Walk from room to room with a notepad or printout in hand. Write down every area that nags at you, such as a pile of shoes by the door, a desk drowning in paperwork, the infamous mail drop where bills and magazines pile up. Trust your instincts here; your frustration is a better guide than any home organization expert. If you have tech-savvy tendencies, you can even snap photos on your phone and create a digital "hotspot album" for reference.

Once you have your map, it's time to decide where to start. Ignore any advice that insists there's only one correct order. Instead, I recommend prioritizing based on emotional impact and daily use. Ask yourself:

- *Which spot makes my life harder every single day?*
- *Which area would give me the most relief if I could wave a magic wand and see it tidy?*

Sometimes it's as humble as the car cupholder, sticky with old coffee receipts and gum wrappers. Other times it's the kitchen counter, a battlefield of school forms, grocery lists, and yesterday's lunchbox. There's no shame in choosing a tiny zone with a big emotional payoff. Tackling a high-traffic area (like the front door drop zone) pays dividends in sanity every time you come home.

Hotspots can be persistent beasts. You clear them out on Sunday afternoon, but by Tuesday evening, someone has deposited their backpack, yesterday's mail, or an odd sock right back where you started. If your family seems determined to refill the kitchen counter no matter how many baskets or labels you try, take heart: you are not alone in this struggle. One trick is to assign everything a home nearby. For instance, you could use hooks for keys, bins for incoming mail, or even a decorative tray for pocket change. Make it easy for everyone (including yourself) to put things away without extra steps. If you live with chronic refiller types (and most of us do), gentle reminders help. A small sign or label ("Mail Goes Here," "Keys Only") can quietly nudge habits in the right direction.

Shared spaces add another layer of complexity, especially if you're not the only one who cares about clutter (or lack thereof). If you share a laundry room with a spouse who thinks socks are best stored on top of the dryer, or have teenagers who believe every step counts as "close enough" to the hamper, it may be time for some negotiation. Try inviting them into the process, not as an order, but as a request for input. Ask what system would make it easier for them to participate: "Would baskets work better than drawers?" "Should we hang hooks instead of folding towels?" Sometimes family members just need an approach that fits their habits rather than your own vision of order.

If certain hotspots persist despite your best efforts, get creative with boundaries. Place a small basket where clutter naturally gathers and agree as a family that when it fills up, everyone spends five minutes putting items away. For high-traffic zones like living rooms and kitchens, designate "clutter catchers." I particularly love stylish bins, trays, or baskets that blend in with the décor instead of looking like punishment. The beauty of this system is that it removes the guilt and finger-pointing. At the end of the day, you just empty them out and start fresh, no drama required. Over time, these little rituals build a family rhythm where everyone shoulders the responsibility

---

To-Do: Clutter Hotspot Map

Try drawing your own Clutter Hotspot Map right now.

1. Start with a quick floor plan; no need for straight lines!
2. Mark each trouble zone with an "X" and jot down what collects there (mail, shoes, coats, gadgets).
3. Circle one or two areas that bother you most—these are your starting points.
4. Keep this map on the fridge or tuck it into your planner as a living document. As one hotspot is tamed, move on to the next. Small victories here will add up to real relief throughout your home.

THE MINDFUL ART OF SWEDISH DEATH CLEANING

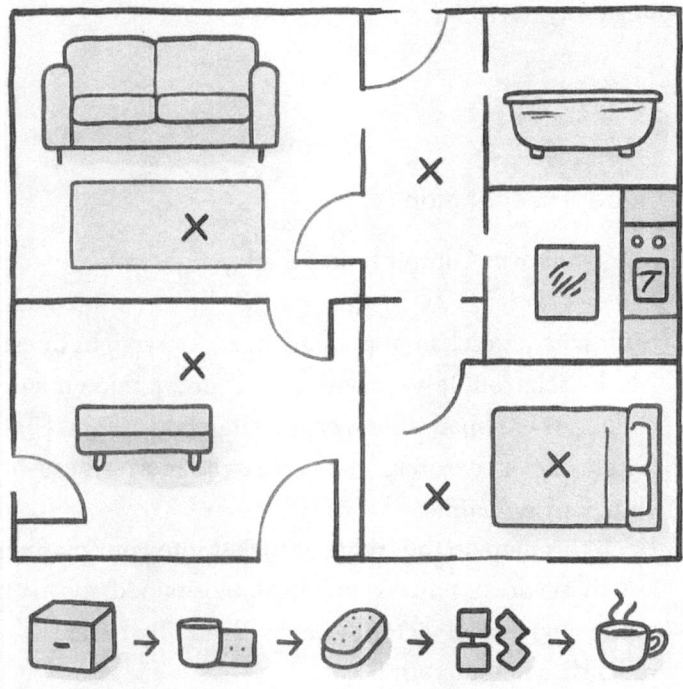

Identifying and mapping your own clutter hotspots won't fix everything overnight. It will, however, give you an honest starting point and a clear sense of direction. Instead of feeling like you have to conquer every mess at once, you'll be able to focus on what actually impacts your peace day-to-day. When you look at your map and see those "X" marks shrinking over time, it'll be proof that progress is happening, even if your family occasionally tries to sabotage it with another pile of shoes or mismatched Tupperware lids.

Decluttering in 10-Minute Intervals

You might think clearing clutter means blocking off an entire weekend, but real progress can sneak into the tiniest pockets of your day. Perhaps your mornings are a whirlwind of work, appointments, and family needs. Maybe your energy dips by late afternoon and the thought of tackling a whole closet makes you want to pull the covers over your head. This is where mini-moments become life-changing. You don't have to move mountains; sometimes, you just need to move one lonely mug out of the cupboard or toss those expired vitamins from the medicine cabinet. You can absolutely declutter in ten-minute intervals, and sometimes, that's all the time or energy you really have to spare.

Think about the last time you waited for water to boil or sat through a TV commercial break. Instead of scrolling or staring at the microwave, grab a small area and give it your focused attention. The goal is not to exhaust yourself, but to chip away at clutter without even breaking a sweat. I often tell women: no marathon sessions required, just a few focused minutes here and there. This approach works for everyone, whether you're busy juggling work and family or just not up for heavy lifting today.

Here's a menu of micro-tasks you can tackle in ten minutes or less:

- Head to the pantry and check those spices. Tip: If the cinnamon expired before your youngest was born, it's time for it to go.
- In the car, open the glove compartment and evict old napkins, mystery pens, and that ancient insurance card.
- Pick a single shelf on your bookcase and pull down anything you haven't read, won't reread, or meant to donate since last summer.

- Bathroom counters are ripe for a quick win: toss expired medications, samples you'll never use, and duplicate lotions.
- Open the utensil drawer in the kitchen and count how many spatulas you really need.
- If you're feeling brave, tackle the sock drawer and say goodbye to singles waiting hopelessly for their mates.

Before you begin, set a timer for ten minutes. When it dings, stop. Don't keep going until you hit a wall! The point is progress, not exhaustion, so stop while you still have energy. Give yourself permission to celebrate these tiny wins. Put a sticker on your calendar every time you finish a ten-minute task. Tell a friend about your victory (extra points if they join you). Do a little happy dance in your kitchen (my personal favorite), or just enjoy that new patch of empty space.

You'd be amazed at how quickly these mini-moments add up. I remember the first time I tried this while waiting for my tea to steep. I managed to clean out my makeup bag during one commercial break and found three tubes of mascara older than my favorite cardigan. No stress, no drama. Just small, steady progress that leaves us feeling lighter every step of the way.

It helps to keep a running list of areas that could use attention, but don't let it become another source of pressure. The beauty of this method lies in flexibility; if today only allows you to sort receipts from your purse or delete old photos from your phone, that's enough. Tomorrow, you may have energy for something bigger. When motivation is low or life feels heavy, just remember that even five or ten minutes can reclaim space for your home, and your mind.

If you enjoy accountability or just like marking milestones, I suggest tracking your mini-moments in a notebook or planner. Each sticker or checkmark is proof that you're moving forward, even if the pace is gentle. Motivation grows when you see those tiny steps turn into real change. The next time you put away groceries or hang up a coat, let yourself notice the difference. Observe how much easier it feels to find what you need and how peaceful it is not to stare down chaos every time you open a door.

Mini-moments are perfect as they honor real life's limits: busy schedules, fluctuating energy, and days when ambition is nowhere to be found. You don't need heroic stamina or hours of free time. You need ten minutes and a willingness to start small, again and again, until progress becomes part of your everyday rhythm. Women who practice this method often tell me it's not just their homes that feel lighter; their mood lifts as well. Suddenly, decluttering isn't another chore but an act of self-respect, a way to claim pockets of calm in a noisy world.

Fika Breaks: Building Swedish Joy Into the Process

In Sweden, "fika" is more than just a coffee break. It's a cultural pause, a deliberate moment to slow down and enjoy the simple pleasure of being present. Whether at work, home, or a café, Swedes gather for fika to savor not only a hot drink but also the joy found in small things. Picture yourself mired in a stack of paperbacks, wondering about your collection; instead of pushing through exhaustion, you pause. You light a candle, play comforting music, brew tea, and have a pastry. This is fika: a sustainable, enjoyable way to work.

Fika's magic is in its invitation to step off the productivity treadmill. It encourages kindness to yourself during the process, not just at the finish line. Emerging in the 18th century, when coffee first took hold in Sweden, fika became a daily ritual for connection and joy. Today, it's typically a mid-morning or afternoon pause for coffee or tea, pastries like cinnamon or cardamom rolls, and an appreciation of the moment. Even prepping for fika by laying out cups, picking a treat, or opening a window signals a time to recharge and savor the present.

You can easily weave fika into your decluttering routine. Before you start, choose a break time and how you'll spend it. Light a candle for atmosphere, prepare your favorite drink, and play music that lifts your mood. The break needn't be long; even fifteen minutes can reset your energy. Step outside for fresh air if you can. These small rituals transform decluttering from drudgery into self-care.

Fika is even better when shared. Invite a declutter buddy (a friend, sister, neighbor) to join you. Work on separate corners, then regroup for coffee and conversation. Sometimes it's half cleaning, half catching up, which is the whole point. If you can't meet in person, do a video call fika: declutter while chatting, then take your pastry break together and trade stories about your finds. Knowing someone else is sorting their "maybes" too lightens the mood and brings laughter into the process.

For those who like to bake (or simply snack) reward yourself with a Scandinavian recipe such as cinnamon buns (kanelbullar). Their aroma can make the work worthwhile, but store-bought cookies are just as good if baking isn't in your plans. The real value is the touch of mindfulness, the gentle act of slowing down to savor what you're eating and notice how much you've accomplished. I like to make fika a tiny celebration after every decluttering milestone: light another candle, use my favorite mug, and even let my pets share the moment (yes, cats enjoy fika breaks, too).

Building fika into your routine simply transforms the atmosphere. Instead of slogging through tasks, you start associating the work with pleasure and comfort. One of my friends actually looks forward to her Friday afternoon fika, because she pairs it with the least glamorous task imaginable: sorting old magazines. She bribes herself with coffee and a homemade scone halfway through, and somehow the job feels less like a chore and more like a treat. She listens to her energy, too; when she hits a wall, she takes a tea break by the window, and it resets her completely.

The truth is, burnout is real when you're tackling years' worth of belongings. You might start with gusto, but without breaks, overwhelm and resentment sneak in fast. Fika pauses are the antidote. They remind us that our well-being matters just as much as a tidy closet or cleared shelf. Instead of bulldozing through, we get to pause, breathe, reflect, and maybe even pat ourselves on the back. Over time, the ritual becomes an anchor, proof that change happens one box, one bag, and yes, one cup at a time.

At its heart, fika is about gentle encouragement. Celebrate the small wins. Find joy in the process instead of punishing yourself for not doing more. And for the love of all things Scandinavian, stop calling breaks "wasted time." They're fuel. Whether you're knee-deep in Christmas decorations or untangling decades-old paperwork, a candle and a warm mug won't fix everything, but they'll soften the hard edges.

Health, Age, and Ability Objections

It's true: health challenges and physical limitations are part of life, no matter your age. If you've ever groaned at the thought of tackling your closet, or felt your lower back twinge just imagining a stack of boxes, trust me—you're in good company. One of the biggest myths about Swedish death cleaning is that there's some magical cut-off date where you're suddenly "too old" or "too tired" to start. I hear it all the time: *"I don't have the strength I used to"* or *"This ship has sailed."* Well, it hasn't. Your timeline is yours alone. Energy ebbs and flows, but the power to reshape your space and the legacy you leave doesn't expire. Even the smallest steps matter, and those small steps stack up faster than you'd think.

Real talk: at fifty-five, my knees are not what they used to be. I've also developed a sincere appreciation for chairs with actual padding. The solution? Smart modifications. They turn "impossible" into "totally doable," and sometimes even enjoyable. Instead of schlepping boxes across the house, I use a rolling cart or a wheeled laundry basket; it's amazing how fast the strain disappears when the wheels clock in. On sorting days, I park at the kitchen table with a box of old letters and work from my favorite chair. No rule says you have to stand and stoop for hours. Sit down, flip on a good lamp, and take your time. And if heavy lifting is off the menu, call in reinforcements: a partner, neighbor, or trusted friend. A decluttering buddy lightens the load and usually brings the laughs.

If you're starting in your seventies or eighties—and truly, go you—you're not at a disadvantage. I've seen the opposite. My aunt Joan recently began Swedish death cleaning at seventy-nine and inspired her entire family by tackling a mountain of photo envelopes one at a time. She kept her favorites, labeled names and dates, and passed the rest along in small batches to her children and grandchildren. No rushing. No marathon weekends. Her secret was consistency: a few envelopes every Sunday afternoon, often with her granddaughter beside her. The process became a gentle ritual rather than a chore, and it never once felt overwhelming.

There's no need for speed or grand gestures. Even five items sorted each week accumulate into real change over months. If you can do more on a good week, wonderful. If not, that's perfectly fine too. Again, give yourself credit for every action taken, no matter how small it may seem. Acknowledge the win when you empty a box or clear out a shelf. Mark it on your calendar or treat yourself to something special.

Fatigue and mobility issues don't mean you're out of the game. They simply ask for a different approach. Use lightweight baskets to gather things that need sorting. Place items on a card table at chair height instead of bending or stretching. Keep pathways clear so you can move safely as you work. For tasks that feel intimidating, break them into parts. Sort half a box today, the rest tomorrow. Give yourself days off without guilt; rest is part of the process.

The beauty of Swedish death cleaning lies in its adaptability. There are no penalties for taking your time or asking for help. You may even find that working slowly allows you to enjoy memories as they surface. Every letter, photograph, or keepsake is an invitation to reminisce without pressure or deadlines.

If motivation falters, remember why you're doing this: to create comfort for yourself now and relief for loved ones later. The end result isn't just an organized space, but peace of mind, freedom from worry about unfinished business, and the satisfaction of knowing you made thoughtful decisions about your belongings.

Every life stage brings its own wisdom and resourcefulness. Perhaps you're good at knowing how to pace yourself, at feeling when it's time to pause or push forward. Keep going at your own rhythm. Consistency trumps intensity every time. You are not racing anyone and there are no gold medals for speed, only rewards for showing up for yourself.

THE ROOM-BY-ROOM SWEDISH METHOD

The Kitchen

The kitchen. Ah yes, the Bermuda Triangle of clutter. Things go in, but they don't always come back out, unless it's via a yard sale or the donation bin. My own "everything drawer" once coughed up three melon ballers (why?), a garlic press I swear I've never used, and an ice cream scoop that looked like it belonged in a Game of Thrones battle scene. If your kitchen has turned into a museum of abandoned culinary ambitions, congratulations—you're normal.

Here's where the Swedes swoop in with their magic word: **lagom.** It means *just enough*, which, thankfully, does not translate to "give up coffee" or "say goodbye to cookies." Lagom is about balance. It's involves keeping the tools that actually serve you and ditching the ones that just eat drawer space. It's the difference between stress-baking cookies while balancing a stack of unopened mail on the counter and joyfully whipping up a batch with your daughter, counters gloriously clear.

You can start with the gadgets. Take a deep breath, channel

your inner fika hostess, and ask yourself: "Do I actually need five cheese graters? Two waffle irons? Three coffee makers?" If the answer is no, be ruthless. Keep what you use monthly. Donate what's good but neglected. Toss the broken, the incomplete, and the suspiciously sticky. Yes, saying goodbye to that quesadilla maker might sting, but trust me: someone else is waiting to give it the love it deserves.

Next stop: the pantry, otherwise known as the graveyard of "just in case" items. Pull it all out (yes, all of it). You'll be amazed how quickly "one bag of chickpeas" turns into eight. Make three piles: keep (fresh and frequently used), donate (unopened and still safe to eat), and toss (expired mystery cans). As you put things back, group them logically: spices together, grains in jars, snacks where you can actually see them. And when you donate that untouched quinoa to the food pantry, give yourself a little gold star! You're decluttering *and* helping someone else. Now that's clutter karma at its finest.

Swedish Pantry Audit Checklist

Quickly audit your pantry in fifteen minutes:

- Remove all dry goods, cans, and spices
- Check expiration dates and packaging
- Group items: grains, beans, baking supplies, snacks
- Set aside unopened but unused goods for donation
- Wipe shelves before restocking
- Keep most-used items within easy reach

Now, focus on the heart of your kitchen, where meals, celebrations, and conversations happen. Organize what remains so it supports daily life, easy cooking, and joyful gatherings. The Swedish "fika tray" tradition is a lovely touch: keep a tidy tray with a teapot, mugs, and cookies ready for spontaneous visits. This means you'll always be ready for guests; no more searching for matching cups. For items that multiply (like mugs and bakeware), apply the "one in, one out" rule: when a new item arrives, donate or gift an old one.

Entertaining stops feeling like a stressful Olympic sport the minute everything in your kitchen has a proper home. Serving dishes live together like happy little roommates, and utensils? They belong right next to your prep area, because no one wants to sprint across the kitchen mid-onion chop. Drawer dividers, baskets, or even an old shoebox (yes, I said it: free organizing!) keep the chaos contained without requiring a second mortgage at The Container Store. And those trendy open shelves are just great for showing off your chic mugs or Grandma's teapot. But if it's not display-worthy, it belongs behind a cabinet door so your counters can actually be used for—shocking twist—cooking.

The kitchen is where people inevitably end up, mostly because it's warm, it smells good... and there's usually wine. Embracing *lagom*, that lovely Swedish vibe of "just enough," means you've got more space for connection, laughter, and maybe even dancing while you stir the sauce. And if one day you find yourself mourning the melon baller you decluttered, take a deep breath. Remember: in Sweden, balance is beautiful, and so is a kitchen that works for your life *today*.

Closets

Closets. Oh, the drama. I don't know a single woman who hasn't stood there, staring at a wardrobe crammed to bursting, and declared with absolute certainty: "I have nothing to wear." It's practically a rite of passage after forty. Truthfully, most of us own way more than we actually wear. Enter the magical One-Year Rule. If it hasn't touched your body in the past twelve months, darling, it's time to set it free.

Here's how you tackle it: pull everything out. Yes, *everything*. Don't you dare try to cheat by leaving that suspicious pile of scarves stuffed in the back. Toss it all on the bed or another clean surface. It will look like a fabric explosion, but chaos is step one. Clarity is step two. Then, sort by season and try on anything that makes you hesitate. Ask yourself the big questions:

Does it fit, or am I still living in the land of "someday it will"?

Do I actually feel good in it, or do I look like I'm auditioning for my own pity party?

Does this match the life I have now, or the fantasy life where I sip martinis at cocktail parties I never go to?

Grab a printable closet tracker and make three columns: *keep, donate, maybe*. The "maybe" pile is where the soap opera plays out, so don't pressure yourself to make final decisions today. Circle back in a week with fresh eyes and less sentimentality.

Here's the golden rule: keep the pieces that make you feel confident, comfortable, and authentically you. If something hangs there whispering guilt ("but it was *so* expensive" or "I should like this"), maybe think of it as a red flag. Your closet should not feel like a thrift store of obligation. In fact, you deserve one that feels like a boutique curated just for you.

Now, clothing often carries stories as rich as any family heirloom. There's the dress you wore to your nephew's graduation, the blouse from your first job interview, or that old band tee from a summer road trip. It's normal to feel sentimental about these pieces. Sit with each one and reflect: Does this garment represent a memory or a version of myself I want to keep close? Sometimes, simply acknowledging the story is enough to let go. For truly special items (a wedding dress, a military uniform, or your child's first sweater) consider a "Farewell Ritual." Hold the piece, remember its story, and perhaps even say thank you aloud before parting with it. If you're comfortable, snap a photo for your memory book.

Letting go isn't always all-or-nothing, either. If parting with a loved piece seems impossible, try creative solutions. Repurposing can breathe new life into old favorites, for instance by transforming a silk blouse into a decorative pillow or sewing patches from cherished shirts into a memory quilt. For items that still have plenty of wear left but no longer fit your style, gifting can be deeply satisfying. That favorite jacket might delight a niece heading to college or bring comfort to a friend who loves vintage finds.

To help maintain simplicity long-term, the capsule wardrobe Swedish-inspired hack will save your mornings (and maybe your sanity). The rule? Ten pieces per season. Yup, that's it. Two pants, three tops, one versatile dress, a skirt, a cozy cardigan, and two pairs of shoes that don't kill your feet. Suddenly, you've got a closet that works for you instead of mocking you every time you try to get dressed.

If you're feeling it, you can stick with a calming palette: navy, gray, beige, white. Basically, the Ikea showroom version of chic. Then, sprinkle in one or two "fun colors" if you can't resist a little pizzazz (we see you, hot-pink scarf). This setup means no more impulse-buy dresses still wearing their price tags three years later. Shopping gets intentional, mornings get easier, and you'll look put-together without the 20-minute meltdown in front of the mirror.

And listen, decluttering your closet doesn't have to erase your style or force you to toss that sentimental concert tee you secretly wear for cleaning days. You're just curating a wardrobe that makes sense for *your life now*. Every piece that stays has earned its spot. Which means less wasted energy, more confidence, and room for new stories.

Bedrooms

A bedroom should be a haven, not a catch-all for life's unfinished business. Yet, it's so easy for these restful spaces to morph into storage zones for paperwork, hobby overflow, or the treadmill that silently judges us from the corner. You deserve a room that supports deep sleep and gentle mornings, not a place where bills or forgotten exercise gear pile up and steal your peace.

Take a clear-eyed look around, and notice any non-sleep-related items that have taken up residence. Exercise equipment, stacks of paperwork, old computers, half-finished crafts: these do not earn their keep by your bedside. Relocate or remove them entirely. Your room's primary job is rest and restoration, not multi-tasking as a gym or office.

When we see a tidy space as we drift off, it signals to our brain that all is well. Unfortunately, nightstands tend to attract the most curious mix of clutter: books you meant to read, tangled chargers, cough drops from two winters ago. It's understandable; this tiny area is the last thing you see at night and the first in the morning. Yet it deserves attention. Empty the drawer and top surface completely. Wipe away dust and crumbs (no judgment; I've found chocolate wrappers and hair ties hiding in mine). Sort through each item, and keep only what you use nightly, like a reading lamp, hand cream, a calming book, or your glasses. Everything else can find a new home or go. A small tray can corral essentials so they don't scatter. Try to limit yourself to three to five items on top.

Swedish bedrooms are known for their calm, airy feel, spaces that whisper, "Take a breath here." The secret is light, neutral colors on walls and bedding, natural wood accents, and just enough decoration to feel cozy without chaos. You don't need to repaint your whole room or buy new furniture. Layering soft linens or adding a wool throw at the end of your bed can do the trick. Swap harsh lights for warm bulbs or add a tiny bedside lamp with a dimmer for evenings. Even one potted plant or a vase of fresh flowers brings in nature's calm. The Danish call this sense of coziness *hygge*, a way of cultivating comfort and presence right where you are.

Instead of scattering mementos on every surface (a ticket stub here, a seashell there) gather your most meaningful treasures into one "memory corner." Select a tray, shelf, or small table and curate just a few items: perhaps a framed photo with your best friend, your mother's watch, or a smooth stone from last year's beach trip. This can become your private sanctuary within the sanctuary, a place for daily gratitude or quiet reflection. Everything else can be stored away or passed along.

Big projects look less intimidating when broken into stages, and there exist helpful methods to keep overwhelm at bay and give us a small win each day. You might not have energy for an all-day overhaul, but five nights of focused effort can transform everything.

Here's a pacing plan that has worked wonders for many women I know:

<u>Monday</u>: Clear and clean the dresser.

<u>Tuesday</u>: Sort nightstands.

<u>Wednesday</u>: Check under the bed (dust bunnies beware).

<u>Thursday</u>: Purge the closet shelf.

<u>Friday</u>: Refresh bedding and add those finishing touches like candles or a favorite pillow.

It's amazing how different a bedroom feels when you remove distractions and focus on restoration. The air seems lighter and mornings feel more hopeful. Even if you share your space with a partner or pets (or both), these shifts support everyone's well-being. The goal is simply to create an environment that welcomes you at day's end and helps you greet each morning with more ease and less stress. A clear room is an act of self-respect, an invitation to rest deeply and rise ready for whatever tomorrow brings.

Attics, Basements, and Storage

If you've ever opened the attic or creaked down basement stairs only to be greeted by towers of boxes labeled "miscellaneous" or "someday," you know that these spaces become museums of our intentions and inheritances. The clutter here feels different from a stuffed closet; it has a certain weight, both literal and emotional. You might find yourself face-to-face with ski boots from 1994, your children's grade school art projects, or your mother-in-law's china set that never quite fit your style. Often, these are the places where "just in case" reigns supreme, and inherited family clutter lies dormant, waiting for someone (usually you) to decide its fate. The most honest question you can ask when you pick up that punch bowl or box of tangled lights is, "Would I buy this again today?" If not, it may be time to bid it farewell.

Sorting the contents of storage spaces can feel daunting, so I rely on the 3-Box Method: one box for items to keep, one for donations, and a third marked "decide later." The "decide later" box is not a trap for procrastination, but a safety net for those things you simply can't part with yet. When you rediscover your child's first teddy bear or a stack of postcards from forgotten vacations, you deserve time to consider. Label the box clearly and set a date to revisit, perhaps after six months or next spring cleaning. This method lets you move forward without forcing rash choices.

Organization is your strongest ally in these sprawling spaces. Gone are the days when every bin was a mystery. Start labeling every box as you sort. Use printable templates with clear categories like *seasonal decor, family history,* and *to review in 6 months.* If you're feeling creative, add color coding: blue for winter holidays, green for gardening gear, red for memorabilia. This may sound like overkill, but future-you will thank present-you when searching for that one box of Halloween costumes or your grandmother's recipe cards. Keep an inventory list taped to the inside of the door or on your phone. Nothing fancy, just a running tally so you don't end up with three boxes all marked "old photos."

Of course, not everything stored away can be easily donated or tossed. Hazardous items like old paint cans, solvents, and batteries require special handling. Check your local government's schedule for hazardous waste collection days. These events take everything from ancient cleaning chemicals to rusty garden pesticides. Old electronics or bikes can often be recycled at designated centers or donated to organizations that refurbish them. It's tempting to tuck such things into a dark corner and forget them for another year, but getting them out responsibly frees up space and relieves mental clutter. For anything truly baffling (vintage filmstrips? A broken accordion?), consult community message boards or online marketplaces, as someone always seems to have a use or wants to turn trash into treasure.

Sometimes what seems like nothing more than a dusty archive turns out to hold treasures. My mother's attic once produced a box of letters, some from relatives I'd never met, others from her childhood pen pals in Sweden. Sorting through these together sparked stories I'd never heard before and connected us across generations. There's something uniquely Swedish about this process: inviting family members for a sorting party, everyone bundled in sweaters, giggling at old photos and oddball souvenirs. We made it less like a chore and more like a celebration by pausing for fika breaks, with coffee and cardamom buns between laughs and discoveries.

Tip Time (a.k.a. Saving Your Future Sanity): Do yourself a favor and slap some giant, can't-miss-'em labels on those boxes, with big, bossy handwriting like: *"Halloween Costumes 1998–2010," "Mom's Letters,"* or the classic *"Review on June 2025."* That way, you're not playing a tragic guessing game six months from now, wondering if "Misc." means tax papers, yarn, or your kid's rock collection.

And listen, there will always be that dreaded "maybe" pile, but don't panic. Just park those in their own little purgatory corner. Decisions don't have to happen all at once; as we've talked about, sometimes our hearts need a slow simmer before we're ready to say goodbye to something.

If your attic feels like too much to tackle, call in reinforcements. A neighbor, a friend, or heck, a couple of local teenagers who think lifting heavy things is a fun way to earn pizza money. Aim for progress with one shelf, one decision, or one dusty memory at a time. And here's the sneaky bonus: every single item you release makes the air a little clearer, your shoulders a little lighter, and sometimes, just sometimes, it even gifts you with a forgotten story that makes you smile and remember why this process is worth it.

Documents and Legacy Drawers

Paperwork has a way of multiplying behind closed doors and inside drawers. If you've ever stood over a teetering stack of folders, receipts, tax forms, and warranties, you know the quiet dread that can creep in. It's easy to put off sorting these piles, but the relief that comes from order is unmatched. I always start by gathering every paper (yes, every last bill and greeting card) and spreading them out where I can see what I'm up against. The first step is to sort into broad categories: personal, medical, financial, legal, and the miscellaneous pile where those "what even is this?" documents land. As you move through each piece, use three choices: shred (for anything with sensitive information you no longer need), recycle (for junk mail, old flyers, outdated manuals), or save (for important records and keepsakes).

A handy reference chart can help you decide what's worth keeping forever. Birth certificates, marriage licenses, wills, and property deeds? Permanent residents of your file. Tax returns? Keep seven years' worth. Bank statements, utility bills, and insurance policies? Only as long as needed for reference or warranty. Shred anything with personal data. Identity theft is real, and there's nothing heroic about clinging to old statements from the 1990s. For sentimental papers like love letters or children's artwork, set aside a memory box; not everything must be practical. If you feel overwhelmed, tackle one category per day. Sorting medical records on Monday, financial documents on Tuesday, and so on makes the process less intimidating.

Now for my one of my favorite Swedish-inspired solutions: the Legacy Drawer. This is not an ordinary junk drawer but a dedicated, organized home for all the crucial documents your loved ones may someday need. In Sweden, it's common to keep a "legacy place" where everything vital lives together: your will, power of attorney forms, medical directives, life insurance policies, property records, passwords, emergency contacts, and even instructions for your favorite recipes or pet care routines. Think of it as the ultimate act of kindness for your family; no frantic searching for Mom's insurance card or wondering where the deed is stashed. You can use a physical drawer with labeled folders or a locked fireproof box for extra security. I recommend a checklist taped inside the drawer: will, POA papers, health directives, birth certificates, Social Security cards, marriage license, insurance details, account logins (written safely), and a contact list of attorneys or financial advisors.

Legacy Drawer Checklist

Tape this right inside your drawer or box for instant peace of mind:

✔ Will (updated and signed)
✔ Power of Attorney documents
✔ Medical directives / Advance care plan
✔ Life insurance policies
✔ Property deeds or mortgage papers
✔ Birth certificates (yours + dependents)
✔ Social Security / Medicare / pension details
✔ Marriage license or divorce papers (if applicable)
✔ Passwords + account logins (stored safely, not scribbled on a sticky note)
✔ Contact list (attorney, financial advisor, executor, key family/friends)
✔ Bank account + investment details
✔ Funeral or memorial wishes (yes, you're allowed to be specific!)
✔ Special instructions (pets, heirlooms, secret chili recipe—whatever matters to you)

Let's talk digital clutter, because I'll bet your laptop's Downloads folder is scarier than that miscellaneous drawer in your kitchen.

Tech tends to make Swedish death cleaning a whole lot easier, and a little less... death-y. You can start by scanning your important documents. Your phone camera is fine, or if you're fancy, your printer might even moonlight as a scanner. File everything in easy-to-spot folders like "Medical," "Legal," "Financial," and "Personal." Bonus points if you don't name things "Final_FINAL_USETHIS.pdf" (we've all done it).

Cloud storage apps like Google Drive or Dropbox are your best friends here. Plus, you can share access with trusted family members, so no one's left panicking over your Netflix login when you're not around to share it. Speaking of logins, do yourself a favor and use a password manager. They're lifesavers. Just make sure you leave instructions in your legacy drawer, because no one wants to solve the mystery of "Which password did Mom use for her bank account?"

And photos. Oh, the photos. If your phone is drowning in 12,000 "IMG_2020" shots, you're not the only one. Sort them by year or event now, and future-you will thank you when you're hunting down that beach trip where your hair actually cooperated.

Here's the thing: clarity saves chaos. My neighbor swears by her legacy drawer. When she had surgery earlier this year, her daughter handled everything with zero drama because every insurance card, medication list, and health directive was right there. No worrying, and no digging through dusty boxes or late-night emergency calls. That's love wrapped in peace of mind.

If you've ever watched family members scramble for documents after losing someone (or gone through it yourself), you know how chaotic it feels. A clear paper system spares everyone stress and confusion at the worst possible moment. That gift of calm organization is lasting.

What to Keep Forever vs. What to Let Go

- **Keep Forever:** Birth/marriage/death certificates; wills and POA; property deeds; Social Security cards; military records; adoption papers; health directives
- **7+ Years:** Tax returns; home improvement receipts (if you own); pension/retirement statements
- **Short-Term (Shred After):** Bank statements (1–3 years); paid bills (after confirmation); expired warranties
- **Let Go:** Junk mail; expired policies; old invitations; duplicate statements

Taming paperwork might never be thrilling, but the sense of relief and the gratitude from your loved ones is undeniable. A well-tended legacy drawer is one of the most loving things you'll ever assemble.

The Garage and Shed

Garages and sheds attract so much clutter. Tools, sports gear, unfinished projects, seasonal items, and hobby supplies inevitably pile up, filling every nook. It's easy to promise yourself you'll sort it all one day, but more often than not, that day gets delayed. With some honesty and a simple system based on your actual habits, you can reclaim these spaces to make them functional and inviting.

A good starting point is to take a complete inventory. Notebook in hand, walk through the area and list everything by category: sports, gardening, automotive, paint supplies, seasonal decorations, crafts. Don't just scan the surface, open bins and peek behind big items. You might learn you have multiple versions of the same tool or hobby gear for activities you no longer do. This exercise isn't about feeling bad; it's about seeing clearly. When everything is in black and white, it's easier to recognize what you need and what's just in the way.

Next up: honesty hour. Look at each item and ask yourself: do I actually use this thing, or is it just taking up emotional real estate? Be ruthless, but kind. That yoga mat from 2012 that still smells like rubber and guilt? The tennis racket you swore you'd learn to use (but secretly hate because, hello, running back and forth is exhausting)? Or those "thoughtful" gifts from relatives that are still in their boxes? If you haven't touched it in years, it's time to release it into the wild. Someone out there will actually give it a second life. You'll get space, they'll get joy. Win-win.

For the things you *do* use, let's not pretend organization is optional. Tools like to live with their own kind, thank you very much.

Hang your garden gear on one wall like a proud display.

Toss car tools into a bin where they won't roll away and attack your ankles.

Stick craft supplies in clear containers.

Pegboards are a total game-changer. Hang it, see it, use it.

Use wall hooks. Tripping over a bike or hose doesn't exactly scream "zen Scandinavian order."

Add labels, my friend. Don't complicate it. Masking tape + marker = future you saying, "Wow, I *am* organized."

. . .

Here's the golden rule: no superhero marathons. Don't tackle the entire garage in one go, and (once again) break it into bite-sized pieces. Sports gear Monday. Gardening tools Tuesday. Craft bins Wednesday. Heck, set a 30-minute timer and call it quits guilt-free.

And let me tell you about my friend's shed glow-up. Once a graveyard for broken shovels, she ditched everything but her favorite trowel and some seeds. Add a pegboard, a tiny bench, and boom: instant sanctuary. Now she potters away in peace instead of dodging rusty rakes. Proof that decluttering creates spaces that actually make you happy.

Inventory Worksheet: Garage & Shed Edition

Step 1: List Categories

Create a master list of everything stored in your garage or shed. Suggested categories:

- **Sports Gear**: bikes, balls, rackets, camping, fishing, exercise equipment
- **Gardening Tools**: rakes, hoes, gloves, soil bags, fertilizers, hoses, pots
- **Auto Supplies**: car tools, oil, spare tires, cleaning products, car care kits
- **Hobby/Craft Items**: woodwork tools, paints, sewing machine, seasonal décor
- **Home Maintenance**: paint cans, spare light bulbs, extension cords, ladders

- **Outdoor/Seasonal**: patio furniture, grills, holiday lights, tents, pool items

Step 2: Usage Assessment
For each item, mark one of the following:

- **Use Often** (weekly/monthly)
- **Rarely Use** (once or twice a year)
- **Never Use** (dust-covered, forgotten, or broken)

Step 3: Decision Prompts

- **For "Never Use"**:
    - Who could benefit? (family, friend, neighbor, donation center, recycling)
    - If broken, is it fixable or should it be responsibly disposed of?
- **For "Rarely Use"**:
    - Is it worth the space it's taking up?
    - Could you borrow or rent instead when needed?
- **For "Use Often"**:
    - Where is the most efficient, safe, and accessible storage spot?
    - Can it be grouped with similar items?

Step 4: Storage Planning
Ideas for maximizing space:

- Wall hooks (bikes, hoses, rakes)
- Pegboards (tools, gardening shears, paintbrushes)
- Clear labeled bins (holiday décor, craft supplies)
- Shelves (auto fluids, paint cans)
- Lockable cabinets (chemicals, sharp tools)
- Rolling carts (small frequently used tools)
- Ceiling racks (seasonal gear, camping equipment)

Step 5: Labeling & Safety

- Use **large, legible labels** or color-coded tags.
- Keep chemicals sealed and out of children's reach.
- Store sharp tools safely (sheaths, hooks, bins).
- Ensure flammables are away from heat sources.

Step 6: Legacy & Sentimental Items

- Do you have family heirlooms or keepsakes in the garage (old fishing poles, trophies, handmade furniture)? Decide: Keep, pass on now, or photograph and let go.
- Label sentimental items clearly with their **story** ("This was Dad's fishing rod—meant for Jason").

Step 7: Accountability & Next Steps

- **Timeline:** (e.g., "Garage clean-out day = next Saturday, 10 AM")
- **Helpers Needed:** family, friend, donation pickup service
- **Action Log:**
    - Items donated: _____
    - Items sold: _____
    - Items trashed/recycled: _____
    - Items kept & organized: _____

Tip: *Take before-and-after photos; you'll be shocked at the transformation, and it helps you stay motivated for the next decluttering project.*

DONATION, DISPOSAL, AND DOING GOOD

Finding the Right Home for Every Item

If we're being honest, donating stuff *should* feel good. But sometimes it feels more like a pop quiz you didn't study for. You're standing in front of a donation bin, holding your old curtains, thinking, *Is this going to help someone... or am I just outsourcing my guilt?*

We've all been there: staring at a pile of "still good" kitchen gadgets or half-decent shoes, wondering where they should go and secretly hoping the answer isn't "the landfill." The good news is we're not here to learn about random acts of dumping. This is a process underlined by intentional generosity. Every item that leaves your hands has the potential to make someone else's life a little easier, or at least a little prettier.

Here's where your Donation Decision Tree comes in. This is like your personal sorting assistant. Each item gets a few quick questions before it earns its next adventure:

1. **Do I use it or love it?** If yes, it stays.

2. **Would a friend or family member want it?**
   (Bonus points if they've actually *admired* it out loud.)
3. **If not, what's next?**
   - Donate it if it's in good shape and could make someone smile.
   - Sell it if it's valuable enough to fund your next spa day or charity donation.
   - Recycle or safely toss it if it's beyond saving (no one wants your cracked salad bowl of unknown origin).

This little flow will keep you intentional, clutter-free, and drama-proof. No more "maybe someday" piles lurking in the hallway. Every object can find a purpose, and you can get the quiet satisfaction of knowing you're doing good, one meaningful goodbye at a time.

Now, every category of stuff has an ideal destination. Good clothing is welcomed at organizations such as Goodwill, or Dress for Success for professional attire to help women entering the workforce. Towels and blankets are prized at animal shelters; gently-used sheets often help domestic violence refuges or hospitals. Kitchenware can go to Habitat for Humanity's ReStores, which help families starting over. For books, libraries may take modern releases, but literacy programs and shelters happily accept children's books and paperbacks. Working electronics should be given to certified recyclers or groups that provide technology access in underserved communities.

For toys and games, children's hospitals and after-school programs often accept clean and complete sets. Furniture is valuable when donated to Habitat for Humanity or local housing organizations; a spare dresser may help someone rebuilding after hardship. Medical equipment like walkers and canes can vastly improve someone's life if donated through local health groups or lending programs.

Community swaps or online groups (like local Facebook or Nextdoor forums) are great ways to connect extra belongings with new owners, without store intermediaries. Sharing photos or descriptions often leads to quick matches and you may hear back about the impact.

Remember, not every charity serves its mission equally. Before loading your car, check the reputation of your chosen group. Trustworthy nonprofits are transparent and share where donations go, and sites like Charity Navigator or GuideStar offer ratings and breakdowns, to help you avoid scams. Be careful with random donation bins in parking lots; some are for-profit and will resell or trash unsellable items. If you're unsure, call ahead and ask about what's accepted and how donations help.

The Donation Decision Tree Checklist

Use this checklist as you sort:

✔ **Clothing:** Clean, good condition? Donate to Goodwill, Dress for Success, or shelters.
✔ **Linens:** Unstained? Homeless shelters, animal rescues.
✔ **Kitchenware:** Still usable? Habitat for Humanity ReStore, refugee groups.
✔ **Books:** In good shape? Libraries, literacy or shelter programs.
✔ **Electronics:** Working order? Certified e-waste recyclers, tech access charities.
✔ **Toys/Games:** Clean, complete? Children's hospitals, after-school centers.
✔ **Furniture:** Safe and sturdy? Habitat ReStore, housing transition groups.

✔ **Medical Equipment:** Intact and sanitized? Senior centers, lending closets.

Always confirm with the recipient before donating, as needs change by season and location.

How to Let Go Without Guilt

Letting go of still-useful items often brings on guilt. Who hasn't hesitated at donating a scarcely-used breadmaker or a lovely sweater that just doesn't get worn? The voice of thrift nags, "Is it wasteful to let this go?", especially after remembering the effort or expense behind the item. Many of us share this discomfort, feeling pangs of regret: "I spent good money on this," or "It still works fine!" This hesitation is normal when faced with parting from things you once valued.

But what if that guilt could be turned into generosity? Your unused breadmaker could brighten someone's kitchen, or your sweaters could ease a chilly commute for another. Giving isn't just about getting rid of things, but about redirecting abundance to where it's truly needed. There's joy in knowing your belongings can start a new life elsewhere.

Every item has a natural lifespan in your home, and passing it on doesn't end its usefulness; it just shifts it. Remind yourself that your money bought not just the item, but the period of use and enjoyment. Releasing things with intention is not irresponsible, it's proof you value resources and want them to be useful. And, whenever guilt arises, gentle self-talk always helps.

The Guilt Trip No One Asked For (and How to Ditch It Gracefully)

When that inner voice starts guilt-tripping you, it's time to talk back with a little kindness. Try some of these self-talk gems next time you feel that "I *should* keep this" tug:

- *I've enjoyed this, and now it's someone else's turn.*
- *Letting go isn't wasteful, it's thoughtful.*
- *I'm not losing value; I'm sharing it.*
- *The joy this brought me doesn't disappear when I donate it.*
- *It's okay that this served its purpose.*
- *Releasing this makes space for what actually fits my life now.*
- *I bought this for the experience and I got it.*
- *Goodbye clutter, hello calm.*

Letting go can be hardest when you feel like you're admitting to a "wasted" investment. Address that feeling by accepting the sunk cost and focusing on gratitude for the experience and use, rather than resentment. With each item you thoughtfully pass on, you're creating space for new opportunities and a more peaceful home. Generosity extends both to others and yourself.

Some possessions will tempt you to hold on out of habit: unopened gadgets, unworn scarves, or gifts from loved ones. When in doubt, pause and ask: does this item genuinely serve me now? If not, let it go kindly, trusting it will be valued elsewhere.

Letting go involves accepting change with compassion for yourself and others. Release what no longer fits, knowing your decision benefits more than your storage space; it can make a difference in many lives.

Donation Day Rituals

Donation Day should feel nothing like a punishment, and everything like a mini festival in your honor. Think of it as a milestone: a vivid, satisfying pause where you notice how far you've come, and you actually let yourself feel proud about it.

Beyond getting rid of things, you're sending them off on new adventures, giving those items the chance to be useful, loved, or spark joy elsewhere. This is your permission slip to reframe the act: not as losing anything, but as a celebration of space reclaimed and burdens lightened. Every bag that leaves is a trophy, a physical reminder that you are lighter, freer, and more in control.

Honestly, I love the idea of turning this into a ritual. Make it fun, give it flair—heck, give it a name. "Freedom Friday." "Letting-Go Saturday." "Stuff-Be-Gone Sunday." Pick something that makes you grin every time you say it, and suddenly decluttering will transform from a dreaded task into a personal achievement.

Prepping for Donation Day doesn't have to eat up your energy. Start by washing or wiping down anything that needs a little freshening up (nobody wants yesterday's dust bunnies or sticky fingerprints). Gather bags or boxes and sort your donations by category: clothes, books, kitchen gadgets, toys. Labeling saves time and helps donation center volunteers sort quickly.

Next, research where your items will do the most good. Local thrift stores, women's shelters, or libraries all appreciate clean, sorted donations. Many organizations even offer pick-up if getting out is tough for you; just check their websites or call ahead.

Here's a quick checklist:

- Clean items (wash, dust, or wipe down)
- Bag and label by type
- Look up donation sites or arrange pick-up
- Load up the car or set everything by the door for easy transport

The magic isn't only in the giving, but in making Donation Day memorable for yourself. Turn on your favorite playlist while you pack up the car. Invite a friend to join you, and turn the drive into a catch-up session. If you're feeling extra festive, bring along some homemade cookies to share when you drop off your haul (and yes, you deserve to eat one yourself). Afterward, treat yourself to a good coffee, a slice of cake, or a little "fika" moment in true Swedish style, a reward for the effort and a signal that this isn't just another chore crossed off your list.

Of course, there's often a twinge of doubt while letting go, especially with things that once felt important. The "what if I need it later?" voice is persistent, but rarely right. For anything you feel hesitant about, try taking a quick photo before letting it go; a digital keepsake can preserve the memory without taking up space in your closet.

Remind yourself gently: it's not wrong to keep an object when it means something real to you, but most things are only missed in theory, not in daily life.

Building this kind of ritual turns decluttering from punishment into progress worth celebrating. If you like ceremony, create a goodbye ritual: wave at your bags as they go or say a silent thank-you for their service in your life.

Next time Donation Day rolls around, notice how much lighter your home (and your heart) feels. The more often you repeat this tradition, the easier it becomes. What starts as an effort quickly turns into a habit, and then into something joyful. You might find yourself looking forward to these little celebrations, not because of the stuff leaving, but because of the fresh space and possibility arriving in its place.

Recycling, Selling, and Special Item Solutions

There's a peculiar satisfaction in finding a "just right" solution for the odds and ends that won't fit into anyone's donation wish list.

Yet, some belongings (electronics, battered textiles, half-empty paint cans) simply can't be left on a neighbor's porch or tossed in a charity bin. Maybe you've already found yourself staring at a pile of castoffs, wondering *Now what?*

Responsibly parting with your stuff is a love letter to your community *and* the planet. But first, you have to know the rules of the recycling game. Check your local recycling center's website or give them a ring to see what they'll take. Some towns even host e-waste days where you can dump your dead gadgets without the shame. Libraries and city halls often jump in on these events too, turning your decluttering into a civic duty moment.

And listen: old phones, laptops, and cords? Do *not* toss them. They're full of metals and chemicals that can turn your soil into a sad science experiment. Batteries and bulbs also deserve VIP treatment, and most hardware stores or big retailers have bins waiting for them.

As for the clothes that are too tragic even for donation (RIP, favorite pajamas), look up textile recycling programs. Many communities repurpose old fabrics for insulation or industrial rags instead of sending them to landfill limbo.

Then there's the hazardous stuff like paint, old meds, and gardening potions from 1998. These require special handling, not "eh, just chuck it." Your local waste management office or pharmacy usually has drop-off days for this toxic crew. It takes five extra minutes but saves your water supply, your conscience, and possibly a few fish downstream.

When it comes to valuable or collectible items, selling is another way to honor both their worth and your time spent curating them. Online platforms like Facebook Marketplace make local selling easy; snap a few clear photos in natural light, write a concise but honest description, and set a fair price after researching similar listings. Potential buyers love knowing why you're parting with something: "moving to a smaller place" or "clearing space for new projects" adds a personal touch.

Consignment shops are perfect for clothing, accessories, or home décor that still have plenty of life left. I recommend calling ahead to learn their policies, as some only take seasonal items or specific brands. For antiques or collectibles, eBay opens access to national (and sometimes international) buyers who might treasure your vintage Pyrex or mid-century lamp. Estate sale companies are useful when facing a houseful of items, especially if you feel overwhelmed by the sheer volume or need professional help with pricing and logistics. These services usually handle advertising and selling in exchange for a percentage of sales, freeing you from haggling over every teacup.

Sometimes, neither donation nor sale is realistic. Maybe the items are too worn, too quirky, or simply not in demand. That's when creativity steps in. Repurposing, or upcycling, breathes new life into things that otherwise would be tossed. Old t-shirts can become excellent cleaning rags, or be cut into strips and braided into colorful rugs. If you have more sewing ambition, patchwork quilts made from beloved clothes provide both warmth and a cascade of memories each time you snuggle up. Single teacups left behind after sets break can find new purpose as charming mini-planters for succulents or as unique homemade candles for gifts. Empty glass jars can become storage for everything from buttons to pantry staples, and mismatched plates can make whimsical bird feeders in your garden when hung with ribbon.

For those truly oddball items (think theatrical costumes, ancient wheelchairs, or extra-long drapery panels) it pays to think outside the usual donation box. Local theater groups often rely on donated costumes, props, and unusual furniture for their productions; one quick call can turn your old prom dress into stage magic. Animal shelters are always grateful for ratty towels or fleece blankets for bedding and cleanups. If you've ever wondered what to do with an antique piano gathering dust in the living room, consider reaching out to community arts programs or music schools; many will arrange pickup if they know it will inspire budding musicians rather than languish unused.

Resource List: Where Else Can It Go?

- **Electronics/Batteries:** City e-waste events, Best Buy drop-offs
- **Hazardous Waste:** Local government collection days, pharmacies
- **Textiles:** Textile bins (check municipal recycling), H&M garment recycling
- **Selling Online:** Facebook Marketplace (local), eBay (national), Poshmark (clothes)
- **Consignment/Estate Sales:** Local shops, professional sale companies
- **Upcycling Ideas:** T-shirts (rags/quilt), teacups (planters/candles), jars (storage)
- **Specialty Donations:** Theaters (costumes/props),

animal shelters (towels/blankets), arts programs (large instruments/furniture)

Finding the right home for every item means thinking beyond default options and matching your castoffs to new needs in your community. Each choice, whether it's responsible recycling, a quick sale online, or creative reuse, reduces waste and extends the story of what you once loved.

When No One Wants It

There comes a point in Swedish death cleaning when you are left holding something that simply will not find a new home, no matter how hard you try. Maybe you've posted in every local group, called the charities, asked around at yoga class, or checked with friends. Still, that faded armchair or the chipped casserole dish stands stubbornly in the corner, as if it resents being left behind. It's frustrating and disappointing. If you ever feel this twinge of failure, please know you're in good company. Some things simply have outlived their usefulness, and that's okay. The world is not waiting to rescue every last lamp or stack of faded towels.

I've had to let go of things that once held a proud place in my home, only to realize their chapter had closed. When this happens, I practice a simple ritual that helps me release the last bits of guilt or regret. I stand with the object one last time and say, perhaps aloud or just in my mind, "Thank you for your service—now it's time to let go." Sometimes I'll snap a quick photo before saying goodbye, to capture the memory without needing to keep the item itself. On rare occasions, I even jot down a short note about what the object meant to me or a story it holds. These tiny acts are not silly; they're a wonderful way to honor your feelings and provide closure. They also allow you to acknowledge the role something played in your life before it moves on.

When it comes down to it, disposing of items is never anyone's favorite part of this process, but sometimes it's the only responsible choice. If you find yourself with bulky things like an old mattress or broken appliances, look into your city's bulk trash days or special pick-up programs. Most towns have designated times when you can leave large items curbside for collection.

The key is to make these choices with awareness and care for the environment wherever possible. I know how tempting it is to toss everything in the trash after a long day of sorting, but taking a few extra steps protects both your conscience and the planet. If you're uncertain about what goes where, most city websites provide clear instructions and schedules.

When all is said and done, focus on gratitude rather than guilt. Your belongings served you, whether as trusty kitchen tools, cozy blankets, or even that plastic plant holder that never quite fit anywhere. Their usefulness has ended with you, but that doesn't diminish their worth while they lasted.

As you clear them out, say to yourself: **"I honor what this object gave me, and I welcome the freedom of letting go."** This affirmation will help rewire your thinking from scarcity and shame to abundance and release.

Remember: You are not obligated to carry every relic into the future. By thoughtfully releasing what cannot be rehomed, you are demonstrating respect for yourself, respect for your needs now and the peace you deserve going forward. Each difficult goodbye is really a hello to more joy, more ease, and more space for what truly matters now.

Avoiding Clutter Creep

After you've worked so hard to clear your home, there's a sneaky culprit that starts creeping back in when you least expect it: clutter creep. This is the gradual, almost invisible, return of stuff after a satisfying cleanout. It happens in small ways: a birthday gift you're not sure about, a cute mug from a friend, or the great deal you couldn't pass up at the store. Sometimes it's boxes from a relative who downsized or inherited pieces from a family member. And clutter rarely marches in all at once; it trickles back through daily life, hiding in shopping bags, mail piles, and the occasional impulse buy. Even with the best intentions, it's easy to find yourself wondering how that tidy shelf became crowded or why your closet feels tight again.

You don't need to feel frustrated or defeated; this is normal and happens to everyone. The key here is to stay a step ahead with conscious habits and a few clever strategies.

One of the most effective defenses is the "one in, one out" rule. Every time you bring in something new (a sweater, kitchen tool, book) commit to letting go of something similar. This simple exchange keeps your space stable and makes you pause before adding more. It also builds awareness around what you truly value because you begin asking yourself, "Is this new thing better than what I already have?" Over time, this becomes second nature.

Another helpful approach is scheduling regular check-ins with your space. Think of this as a mini-declutter session. Set aside time each month or season to quickly review high-traffic areas like entry tables, bathroom cabinets, or the kitchen counter. Many find it easiest to tie these mini-sessions to natural transitions: the start of a new season, a holiday changeover, or just after a birthday when new gifts arrive. Use a checklist for these reviews, jotting down hotspots like under the bed, the junk drawer, your purse, and your car's glove box. It doesn't take long, and just ten minutes per area can prevent weeks of future frustration.

Even more powerful than routine is **building new habits that create pause points** before things cross your threshold. When tempted by a store display or an online sale, stop to ask yourself:

Do I truly need this?
Does it have a space in my home?
Does it have space in my life?

If the answer isn't clear or you're hesitating, consider waiting. Often, just walking around the store once or leaving an item in your online cart for 24 hours helps break the spell of impulse. Another trick is to keep a "maybe" box for incoming items. Place new purchases or gifts there for a set period, maybe two weeks, and see if you reach for them or forget they exist. If you don't use them during that trial time, they probably aren't necessary.

I've met women who could teach a masterclass in creative clutter control. One of my favorites comes from a friend who turned her birthday into Donation Day. Instead of collecting more scented candles and novelty mugs, she invites her friends and family to join her in rounding up stuff they no longer need. Everyone goes home lighter, the local charity gets a boost, and she doesn't have to fake enthusiasm over another bath bomb set. Win-win.

Another family I know has an annual post-holiday ritual: every January, they gather to sort through their decorations. Anything cracked, faded, or just plain creepy gets the boot. Only the meaningful pieces stay. The result is a joyful attic, a stress-free decorating day, and zero guilt when the silly season ends and the snowman retires.

Now, sustaining a clutter-free home doesn't mean never accumulating anything new, but making intentional choices and staying aware of what comes in and what goes out. You might find it helpful to jot down your own list of common clutter triggers: free samples from events, hand-me-downs from relatives, grocery store promotions. The more you notice these patterns, the easier it will become to pause and decide if each item deserves a place in your life.

You may also want to engage your household by sharing these strategies openly and inviting everyone to participate. Post your mini-declutter checklist on the fridge, involve kids in regular toy reviews, or team up with a spouse for monthly closet edits. When everyone feels invested in keeping things tidy and light, maintenance feels less like work and more like mutual care.

Over time, these tiny habits really do stack up. Before long, your home will feel lighter, fresher, and calmer, like it finally took a deep breath. Sure, you'll slip up occasionally. Everyone does. But clutter doesn't judge, and neither should you. Just pick your favorite habit, jump back in, and start fresh. No shame, no drama; just you, creating a life with a little more space to breathe.

BOOK III

BOOK III

The Heart:

Letting Go, Healing, and Passing Down Legacy

PRESERVING WHAT MATTERS

You know that moment when you open a box labeled "Treasures" and find a mismatched set of salt shakers, a faded apron, and a brooch shaped like a squirrel? If you're like me, you might pause, laugh, and then wonder: is any of this actually an heirloom, or am I simply the last stop before the thrift shop?

The truth is, not everything that survives a few decades deserves to be called an heirloom. Yet, sorting the meaningful from the merely old can feel like emotional gymnastics, especially when nostalgia and guilt start competing for your attention.

Let's make this easier and give you some clarity. First, a true heirloom carries more than age; it carries emotional resonance, a story, or a tradition that links generations. Think of your grandmother's wedding ring or the recipe book with notes scribbled in the margins. These items are unique, woven into your family's narrative, and irreplaceable. A hand-me-down, on the other hand, is usually just useful or sentimental for a season. Maybe it's a casserole dish you inherited because nobody else wanted it, or a set of towels that have quietly traveled from house to house without fanfare. Both have value, but only one truly shapes your legacy.

Sometimes, usefulness tips the scale. Your father's favorite carving knife may be passed down for practical reasons as much as sentiment. But for most items, emotional value and uniqueness are what elevate them to heirloom status.

To help you sort out what's worth keeping for posterity and what can move on, try using a decision matrix with these guiding questions:

- Does this item hold a family story or tradition?
- Would I want to receive this myself?
- Is it unique or one-of-a-kind?
- Is there someone specific who would appreciate it?
- Does it still serve a purpose or bring joy?
- Would letting it go erase something truly important?

If you answer "yes" to most of these, then you may have an heirloom on your hands. If not, you're more likely to be holding onto something out of habit or fear of regret.

Your Heirloom Decision Matrix

Take out a notebook and list five items you're unsure about. For each one, answer the above questions honestly. You might be surprised: sometimes the object you thought was precious is just an old vase with no backstory. Circle the ones that truly matter and note who might cherish them next.

Now, let's talk family. So often we assume our children or nieces want what we've kept safe for years. The reality? Sometimes they don't want anything that can't fit in a backpack. Before declaring an item an heirloom-in-waiting, have an honest conversation. Ask:

Would you want this someday?

Does this remind you of our family in some way?

What do you remember about this piece?

If your loved ones aren't interested (which happens more than we care to admit) it's not a rejection of you or your memories. It's simply life moving forward. In those cases, honor the object another way. Take a photograph to create a collage of "almost heirlooms" that meant something to you, even if they didn't find a new owner in the family. Display this collage somewhere meaningful to remind you that memories can live outside of boxes.

For those items that don't make the heirloom cut but still tug at your heartstrings, consider donating them with intention. Historical societies often cherish unique pieces from everyday life, like vintage aprons or old tools, because they tell stories about ordinary people. Some themed charities welcome collections such as costume jewelry, which can become art projects for children or be sold to support community work.

And if you're not quite ready to let go without ceremony, you could write a farewell letter to the object. Thank it for its role in your life, recall a memory it holds, and wish it well on its next adventure. This small act can transform letting go from loss into gratitude, a gentle closure for both you and your keepsake.

Preserve only what matters; keep what connects you to who you are and where you come from.

Your Legacy Inventory

Okay, this is where the rubber meets the road. The *Legacy Inventory Worksheet* is basically your secret weapon against family squabbles over the good china, and your insurance policy that the stories behind your treasures don't vanish into thin air.

Here's the deal: memories fade, and once we're not around to tell them, even the most cherished keepsakes can turn into useless objects with zero backstory. This worksheet solves that. You'll jot down each item, the story behind it, and your official "pass-it-on" plan. That way, Aunt Evelyn's locket isn't mistaken for some thrift-store find, and your voice and history stick around for good.

Don't do this alone, unless you're actively auditioning for "World's Saddest Solo Decluttering Show." Get your people involved. Invite family over, bribe them with snacks, or hop on video calls if they're scattered across the map. Laugh, cry, and argue lovingly over who *really* broke that vase in 1997. These conversations turn the process into a memory-making event of its own.

Snap a quick picture of each item with your phone and plop it into the worksheet. Photos make everything crystal clear, add context, and, honestly, make the worksheet feel more alive.

So, pour a glass of wine (or tea if you're feeling wholesome), grab your worksheet, and start writing your family's living history, one keepsake at a time.

Getting started is easy: Print out several worksheets, one per room or category, if it helps. Take your time, jotting down memories as they surface. There's no right or wrong way; sincerity always matters more than style. If you're not sure where to start, ask yourself:

Who did I first see using this?

What event does this belong to?

What lesson or feeling do I want this item to pass on?

Even a sentence starting with *This reminds me of...* can unlock treasured details.

Connecting stories to objects blends context, emotion, and identity. When future generations hold an heirloom and read your words, they will inherit love and history, not just things. Your voice lingers each time the worksheet is read or a keepsake is passed along.

Organizing Photos

Sorting through decades of photos can feel like time travel... with jet lag.

Many of us have boxes and albums (some threatening to burst at the seams), envelopes from long-gone photo labs, and a few stray pictures stuck to the bottom of drawers. The hardest part is usually knowing where to begin. I like to start with the simplest step: grouping. Gather every loose print, photo album, and packet you can find onto a large table or the floor. Then begin grouping by decade, major event, or even by person—whatever feels most natural. For instance, one pile might be vacations in the 90s, another your daughter's birthdays, another all those school portraits with the same forced smile but different haircuts. The goal is to create manageable categories.

Once you have your main groups, begin sorting within those piles. Weed out duplicates (who needs five copies of a blurry picnic?), and set aside any photos where you can't identify anyone or anything. If you're feeling ruthless, toss them; if not, create a "mystery" envelope and revisit it later with family. For long-term safety, transfer your favorites into acid-free boxes or albums. Acid-free materials keep photos from yellowing or sticking together over time. It's a small investment that protects your memories for decades more. Then, label each container clearly by decade or event so you (or anyone else) can find what they're looking for later.

The next step is digitizing, which sounds more intimidating than it is. If you have a home scanner, use it to scan photos one by one or in batches. Even a good smartphone camera works in a pinch; just find bright natural light and snap away. There are also local printing shops and online services that will handle large batches for you at reasonable prices.

As you digitize, use a simple yet clear naming system for each file, for example:

- 1996_SkiTrip_Lisa.jpg
- 1985_Anniversary_MomDad.jpg

Consistency matters much more than cleverness here, and future-you will thank present-you for keeping things straightforward.

Digital photos deserve as much care as prints, especially since they multiply faster than rabbits. Create folders on your computer or cloud storage based on year, event, or family member, whatever matches how your brain works.

You will want to aim for clarity over complexity, and several affordable and user-friendly apps can help: Google Photos offers automatic sorting and facial recognition, while Apple Photos syncs easily across devices. For extra security, back up everything in at least two places: a cloud service like Dropbox or Google Drive, plus an external hard drive stored in a safe spot.

Photos deserve to be seen, not trapped in boxes or buried deep in digital folders. One of my favorite ways to bring them into daily life is to create a family slideshow for reunions or holidays. Nothing sparks stories faster than old hairstyles on the big screen! If you enjoy crafts, print a "legacy photo book" using one of the many online services that let you design custom albums; these make heartfelt gifts and keep memories alive for children and grandchildren who may never flip through a shoebox of prints. Another idea is to designate a "Photo of the Month" wall, either a physical frame you swap out regularly or a digital photo frame that cycles through favorites automatically.

These small rituals make remembering easy and joyful. You'll find that sharing photos often leads to sharing stories that might otherwise be lost as people move, grow older, or simply forget the details behind each frozen smile. Even if you only organize your top twenty favorite images, those moments will be easier to revisit and share. And should you ever face a situation where someone asks for a picture of Grandma or wants to see what your first house looked like, you'll know exactly where to look.

If you need an extra nudge to get started or keep going, here's a simple checklist to keep taped inside your photo box:

- ✔ Gather all prints and albums
- ✔ Group by decade/event/person
- ✔ Weed out duplicates and mystery shots
- ✔ Store favorites in acid-free boxes/albums
- ✔ Scan and name digital copies
- ✔ Sort digital photos into clear folders
- ✔ Back up in at least two places
- ✔ Share: slideshow, photo book, wall frame

PRESERVING WHAT MATTERS

Creating a Family Memory Night

If the thought of sorting through dusty keepsakes alone makes you want to fake your own disappearance, I've got a better plan: make it a party. A Family Memory Night turns decluttering into something that actually feels... fun. (Yes, I said it.) It's part nostalgia trip, part comedy special, and entirely worth it for the stories that tumble out; some heartwarming, some horrifying, all 100% family gold.

Start with invitations that feel like an event. Go old-school with real paper cards if you're feeling fancy, or drop a sassy group text. Tell everyone it's a night for stories, snacks, and a little sentimental chaos. Choose a night when no one's rushing off anywhere, and set the mood with twinkle lights or candles that say, *we're classy but not trying too hard*. Add fika-worthy treats (Swedish cinnamon buns are basically required by law), a pot of tea or something stronger, and a few tissues for when the laughter gets teary.

Here's the really special part: everyone brings one object or photo that means something. It could be Dad's hideous fishing hat, Aunt Maggie's disco-era sunglasses, or a concert ticket you swore you'd never throw out. Gather in a circle or around the table, and take turns doing a mini "show and tell." Encourage everyone to spill the story behind their item: how it came to be, who else remembers it, or what kind of mischief was involved. You'll find that once one person starts sharing, the memories snowball. Suddenly you're knee-deep in "Remember when...?" and nobody wants the night to end.

To keep the vibe light (and stop the kids from sneaking off), it's a good idea to add a few games. Try "Memory Bingo" with prompts like *First Pet Story* or *Funniest School Memory*. For the grown-ups, a "story circle" works wonders. Everyone tells one short, funny, or touching story sparked by an old photo. Even your quiet cousin will have something to say after round two of cinnamon buns.

Designate a family historian, a person who's either great at note-taking or dangerously fast with their phone. Have them jot down highlights, record little snippets, or set up a voice memo app for storytime (with permission, of course). Put out Memory Cards where people can write their anecdotes or well-wishes for future generations. Toss them in a pretty basket in the center of the table, which will look nice and give the night a sense of occasion.

And don't forget photos! Capture the chaos of people laughing, holding up odd trinkets, or dramatically reenacting events from 1993. Later, compile it all into a shared album or a digital scrapbook. When you scroll through it later, you'll be amazed at how much love (and questionable fashion) your family history holds.

If you're the organized type (or just love a good project) create a Legacy Binder. Fill it with the recipes served, photos from each night, and hilarious notes like "Uncle Bill's potato salad: still controversial." This binder will become your family's living time capsule, passed around or copied for everyone to keep.

Digital Legacy: Passwords, Files, and Social Media

You probably remember when keeping track of family history meant safeguarding a shoebox of photos and a few important papers in a desk drawer.

Of course, life has changed.

Now, your memories, finances, personal notes, and even family news might be scattered across countless emails, social media profiles, cloud drives, and shopping accounts. It's modern life: convenient but also chaotic.

Digital assets include everything from your email inbox to your Pinterest boards, online banking, cloud photo albums, DNA test results, and even those quirky usernames you made up in 1999.

Think about each place you save memories or handle daily life: email accounts, social media, cloud storage, online banking and investments, shopping logins, streaming services, and the long-forgotten blog about succulents you started one winter. It adds up fast! Most people underestimate how many digital footprints they leave behind. But these footprints can turn into landmines for loved ones if there's no clear map.

The best way to start is to create a master list of your digital world. Begin with the obvious: email addresses and main passwords. Then move to social media, cloud accounts, subscriptions, and any digital wallets or rewards programs. Don't forget devices: phone lock codes, tablet passcodes, laptop logins. It's tempting to jot down everything on loose scraps of paper. Please resist that urge! Instead, use a secure password manager (something like LastPass or 1Password) to store account details safely. These tools let you keep everything encrypted and accessible with one master password (just don't forget that one!). If you prefer paper backup, you could create a printable sheet with space for each account name, login hint (never write the actual password), recovery email or phone number, and short instructions ("delete after I'm gone," "archive for family," "close account"). Store this document in a locked file box or safe with the rest of your legacy papers.

Here's a simple Digital Legacy checklist to help you get started:

✓ List all email addresses and main online accounts.
✓ Note the main device passwords.
✓ Record cloud storage locations and access instructions.
✓ Include instructions for social media profiles (close, memorialize, or keep).
✓ Identify which financial or shopping accounts must be closed or transferred.
✓ Add a trusted contact for each account who can help later.

Now for the tough part: deciding what should stay alive online and what should be erased.

Pause for a moment and ask yourself:

Which accounts would actually matter to your loved ones?

Does anyone need access to your online banking or utility bills?

If you have a blog full of family recipes or a private Facebook album with baby photos, those may be precious. On the other hand, the subscription to a long-defunct newsletter can probably be deleted. For social media profiles, most platforms now offer an option to memorialize or delete accounts after death; Facebook lets you appoint a "legacy contact" who can manage your page. Some platforms require proof or special forms, so gather that info now and add it to your Digital Legacy List.

Communicating your digital wishes is as important as organizing your physical keepsakes. You don't need a formal legal document for every password, but it helps to write clear instructions. Consider drafting a short digital will, just a letter attached to your other important papers, outlining who should access each account and what actions they should take ("archive my photos," "close my Twitter"). Appoint one person as your "digital executor," someone tech-savvy in the family or a trusted friend who can follow these steps without panic. Tell them where your lists are kept and make sure they understand your choices.

Of course, never include full passwords in plain sight. Use hints only you and your trusted person would understand ("my favorite vacation spot + year I married"). Avoid sharing sensitive info via email or text. If possible, update your main digital list at least once a year, or whenever you change major passwords or add new accounts.

Save your family from hours of confusion and frustration while also protecting cherished memories from being lost forever in cyberspace. A little time spent organizing now means your digital life won't become an unsolvable puzzle later.

FAMILY, FRIENDS, AND TRICKY CONVERSATIONS

How to Explain Death Cleaning to Skeptics

Mentioning "Swedish death cleaning" at a book club can certainly raise eyebrows. My friend Julie once joked, "Is this about getting rid of people, or just the ugly vase I gave you ten years ago?" The term certainly invites confusion, even though the reality is much more ordinary and generous than most expect. There's no impending doom or farewell tour of your belongings; we're truly just making life lighter for everyone.

If people are hesitant, gently reframe it as thoughtful preparation rather than a gloomy task. You might say, "Think of it as spring cleaning with a legacy twist." Like Swedes tidying before celebrations, you're creating order to welcome new life stages or experiences: a fresh phase, a move, or simply more clarity at home. There's nothing morbid. Really, it's closer to planning a nice surprise than a somber event.

When explaining to skeptics, analogies can help. Compare it to clearing your closet before shopping, or say, "I'm just doing a little

Swedish housekeeping, making things easier before anyone else has to." If someone finds it macabre, lighten the mood: "No coffins involved! I'm just ready for less hassle and more joy in my space." Humor always helps ease discomfort.

Emotional objections may come up, especially from loved ones who find the idea alarming or unnecessary. Here are a few gentle one-liners to keep in handy:

"I know it sounds dramatic, but in Sweden, it's just being thoughtful."

"No, I'm not planning my funeral! I'm just organizing so there's less stress for all of us."

"This isn't about rushing anything; I'm simply organizing now so nobody else has to later."

"Just as Swedes tidy before a celebration, I'm preparing for what's next."

"This is my gift to myself and to you: a less stressful future."

"Remember me for my laugh, not my boxes of mystery cords."
"It's Swedish tradition with some self-care."

"I'm editing my life story by keeping what matters, and letting go of what doesn't."

Focusing on what you're keeping rather than just what's leaving can transform the conversation. Stress the positives: preserving stories, freedom, and clarity, and most importantly, acting out of love for your family and yourself. As organizing expert

Sarah Giller Nelson notes, Swedish death cleaning gives you control over your story and eases the burden on loved ones.

Conversation Starters for Adult Children

A few years back, my good friend and neighbour found herself standing in her hallway, holding a box full of her son's childhood trophies, tiny golden baseball players and lopsided ribbons that once felt like treasures. There she was, stuck between "keep forever" and "toss immediately (but live with the guilt)." The real problem? How to bring it up with him without sounding like she was literally throwing away his childhood.

When she approached me with this dilemma, I gently reminded her:

> Keep it light, keep it open.

I would say something like, *"Hey, I'd love your input on a few things I've saved from your childhood. Want to go through them with me?"* This makes the conversation feel warm rather than pushy. And since her adult kids' calendars often make hers look like a vacation brochure, I suggested adding a little out: *"If now's not a good time, no pressure. I can set them aside for you to look at later."*

It's a respectful approach, it puts the choice in their hands, and it keeps the whole process from feeling like you're staging an emotional ambush in the middle of the hallway.

Topics like inheritance, memorabilia, or family traditions can make anyone uncomfortable. That's where gentle little scripts come in handy. They keep the conversation soft, kind, and drama-free. A favorite opener of mine is: *"Is there anything here that you'd want someday, or should I find it a new home?"* That way, you're not guilting anyone into taking Grandma's quilt they secretly hate.

FAMILY, FRIENDS, AND TRICKY CONVERSATIONS

Here are some simple, no-pressure phrases you can keep in your back pocket for these conversations:

What do you remember most fondly from our home?

Would this mean something to you, or should I find it a loving new home?

When you think of our family traditions, which things feel the most special to you?

Do you see yourself wanting this someday, or is it better that I pass it along now?

What's one thing from our home that makes you smile every time you see it?

I'd love to know what items carry the happiest memories for you.

If you could choose just one keepsake, what would it be?

Do you want this to stay in the family, or should I bless someone else with it?

What reminds you most of our time together here?

If your children are uninterested in reminiscing or sorting through things, that's normal. Don't take it to heart. If they're too busy or distant, try: "No pressure, just let me know if there's anything you feel strongly about." This removes urgency, letting them decide in their own time. Radio silence isn't a sign of a bad relationship; sometimes life is just hectic.

For sentimental items (baby shoes, handmade cards, a macaroni necklace) be honest about your feelings too. Say, "This one makes me smile every time I see it, but I want you to have it if you'd like." Sometimes adult children worry about hurting your feelings if they don't want something. Reassure them with, "It won't hurt my feelings if you don't want any of this; I just want these things to go where they'll be appreciated." Permission to say no is as meaningful as permission to accept. With family traditions or heirlooms, clarify there's no expectation: "There's no obligation to take anything just because it's been in the family forever." If they are interested in an item, you can offer to write down its story for added meaning and to preserve history.

And if the idea of sorting through everything at once feels like climbing Everest in house slippers, simply break it down. One drawer. One box. One shelf. By inviting your kids into this process, you'll learn what really matters to them, and you'll free up space for fresh beginnings. Even if they only walk away with a handful of treasures, the whole experience can still be meaningful—and dare I say, even a little fun—when you mix honesty with a splash of humor.

The "Claim Your Stuff" Letter Template

I know firsthand how awkward it can feel to reach out to family and friends about old belongings. It's tempting to just leave the boxes quietly in the attic, but experience has shown me that a little communication up front saves a mountain of confusion later.

That's where a simple, heartfelt *Claim Your Stuff* letter comes in. This isn't a legal summons or a guilt trip; it's more like sending out an invitation to a quirky family treasure hunt. I like to start with warmth and a dash of humor, stating that I've come across some treasures (and maybe a few oddities) that I'd love for them to look through. This sets a friendly tone and lets everyone know there's no pressure, just an opportunity.

The beauty of this approach lies in its flexibility. You can send the message by email, old-fashioned letter, or even a group text; whatever fits your crowd best. I recommend personalizing it with details that remind your loved ones they're welcome to say yes or no. For example, "No obligation, just let me know if anything sparks a memory or a smile." This takes away any sense of duty and turns the process into an invitation for connection. Setting a gentle deadline keeps things clear: "I'm giving everyone until [date] to speak up. After that, the donation box awaits!" Without a time frame, these things tend to linger forever, and nobody needs another indefinite project.

I've learned that being explicit about what will happen to unclaimed items prevents hard feelings down the line. A simple line like, "If I don't hear from you, I'll assume you're happy for me to pass things on to others who need them," gives you freedom to move forward and lets everyone know the plan. It closes the loop so that, months later, nobody can pop up asking about the fate of their third-grade science fair ribbon.

It helps to get creative with your subject lines in emails or texts; something playful is far more likely to get attention than "Important Family Business." I've sent notes titled "Family Heirlooms Up for Grabs!" and "Claim Your Childhood Relics—Last Call!" People are much more likely to open a message that sounds like fun. In the body of your letter, list out categories or special items you've come across: "Old yearbooks, mystery kitchen gadgets, and at least one lava lamp await you." This sparks curiosity and makes it easier for recipients to picture what's on offer.

My own attempts with this method have led to some lovely outcomes. Once, my niece responded within minutes of my email, thrilled at the chance to reclaim a childhood book she'd forgotten existed. We ended up flipping through its pages together and laughing over doodles in the margins, and an ordinary afternoon turned unexpectedly sweet. Another time, my cousin called just to thank me for remembering his love of model trains, and we reminisced about hours spent building tiny villages on my living room floor. These little moments have shown me that inviting loved ones into your decluttering process can actually deepen relationships rather than strain them.

When you send out your *Claim Your Stuff* message, think about adding a personal touch for each recipient if you have the energy. Mentioning a specific item ("There's a blue sweater I always remember you borrowing") makes people feel seen and valued. For larger families or groups of friends, you might want to attach photos (nothing fancy, just quick snaps on your phone) to help jog memories and save time.

Crafting boundaries is key. If you have limited space or time, be honest: "I'll need to clear this area by [date], so let me know what you want by then." If someone requests an item but never comes to get it, decide in advance how long you'll hold it before passing it along elsewhere. You're not running a free storage facility; your home deserves peace too.

It's remarkable how such a simple gesture can transform the process from overwhelming obligation to something almost celebratory. Even if not every item finds a new home within the family, you'll have given everyone the opportunity and avoided misunderstandings. And if no one claims Aunt Edna's porcelain cat collection? Well, at least you tried, and maybe someone at the charity shop will fall in love with it all over again.

Navigating a Reluctant Spouse or Partner

Not everyone in a household will share the same relationship to possessions, and few things test this more than the moment you announce you're ready to tackle the basement, or suggest the garage could use "a little Swedish inspiration." It isn't rare at all for one partner to feel energized by the idea of streamlining while the other seems to have both feet firmly planted in the land of "let's not touch my stuff." Sometimes it's simply a matter of personality: one of you clings to sentimental trinkets, and the other would happily live with only five shirts and a coffee mug. Sometimes, it's about deeper attachment styles or how each of you defines comfort, security, or even identity through objects. I've witnessed couples almost come to blows over a stack of faded band t-shirts or a perfectly functional but ancient coffee grinder.

The most important first step is approaching the conversation with curiosity instead of confrontation. Instead of launching into what needs to go, start by inviting your spouse to participate in a way that feels collaborative, for instance by saying "I'd love your help in deciding what to do with these things. Would you be willing to pick one area to start with me?" This approach lowers defenses and frames the project as something you're doing together rather than something you're imposing. Give your partner space to express opinions about what matters, and ask questions such as "Is there anything you feel strongly about keeping or letting go?" This signals respect and eases the pressure. Sometimes, simply knowing their voice will be heard is enough to turn resistance into cautious cooperation.

Creating shared goals can also transform decluttering from a source of tension into an exercise in teamwork. Instead of focusing on what each of you will lose, try setting a positive target: maybe it's making room for a reading nook, clearing space for hobbies, or just being able to find things without a treasure map. Celebrate milestones together. After finishing a closet or clearing out storage bins, reward yourselves with a favorite dinner, a movie night, or even just a walk where no one talks about stuff at all. These rituals reinforce progress and show that you're on the same side. If your spouse needs a little lighthearted encouragement, you might even create playful challenges: whoever clears the most bookshelves gets to pick takeout for the evening.

Now, boundaries are non-negotiable when it comes to shared and individual belongings. It's healthy to establish zones in the home. This respects both autonomy and attachment. If your partner collects tools, vinyl records, or a library's worth of mystery novels, those items can live in their designated area, untouched by your urge to purge. In turn, you get to curate your own spaces without interference.

Sometimes compromise looks like agreeing not to mention certain collections for a set period, or offering to let your spouse choose a few "sacred" items while you do the same. An honest conversation might sound like, "I know your record collection is important to you, and I promise not to make any decisions about it without you. In exchange, it would mean a lot if you could help me sort through these linens I've been avoiding." These small agreements make all the difference.

You may also find that leading by example is remarkably persuasive. When your partner sees the calm that comes from an organized closet or the satisfaction of rediscovered treasures, they may gradually warm up to the idea, even if they never become as enthusiastic as you. It's okay if progress is slow or uneven; what matters is keeping communication open and tempers cool.

If things get heated, take a breather—no pile of old jackets is worth an argument. Remind yourselves that possessions aren't more important than peace at home. And above all, give each other permission for imperfection; sometimes the best you'll achieve is a truce over where the mugs go or who gets which shelf in the garage.

FAMILY, FRIENDS, AND TRICKY CONVERSATIONS

Reflection Exercise: Map Your Shared Space

1. Grab a sheet of paper and sketch out your main living areas together.
2. Mark which spaces are shared and which are "yours," "mine," or "ours."
3. Talk through what feels negotiable and what's off-limits for each person.
4. Use colored pens or sticky notes if it helps visualize boundaries.
5. Agree on one shared area to tackle first and set a small goal, like clearing one shelf or one drawer, before moving on.

This exercise is a perfect reminder that every partnership thrives on patience, humor, and clear communication, even when surrounded by boxes of who-knows-what.

Handling Pushback

Sometimes, even with the best intentions, decluttering sparks disagreement within families. You may find yourself facing sharp words or stony silence from someone who feels your decisions came out of nowhere, or who thinks you're acting too quickly. When I first began sorting through my mother's linens, my sister accused me of trying to erase the past. I'll never forget the look on her face as she clutched a faded tablecloth, certain I was casting off memories instead of fabric. In that moment, I realized that calm, open-hearted words matter more than any organizing tip. Instead of matching her intensity, I took a breath and said, "I understand this feels sudden, but I've put a lot of thought into what matters most to me." That simple sentence opened the door for her to share what she wanted to keep, and for me to show that this wasn't an attack on our shared history.

Disagreements about possessions can go from zero to soap opera really quickly if no one hits the pause button. When you feel the temperature rising, it's perfectly fine (actually, smart) to step back and call a timeout. A breather gives everyone a chance to cool off, check their emotions, and remember that this isn't about winning a battle over an old tea towel. The real goal? Protecting your relationships and honoring the love that got you here in the first place. And sometimes, just saying out loud, "Hey, this feels a little charged right now," is enough to reset the mood. It reminds everyone that you're not cleaning house out of convenience, but doing so from a place of care.

Occasionally, consensus just isn't possible and agreeing to disagree might preserve the peace. In these situations, it's perfectly healthy to set boundaries and let differences stand. You don't have to convince everyone or get unanimous approval; you need only clarity in your own heart and kindness in your delivery.

Families thrive on compromise. A woman in my decluttering group told me her daughter begged her not to donate childhood toys, but her small apartment couldn't hold everything. They made a deal: her daughter picked three special items to keep, and together they donated the rest to a children's charity. The process took negotiation, a little laughter, some tears, but both ended up feeling heard.

If you need space from the conflict, take it. Allow yourself time to think before deciding. Sometimes walking away for a day lets everyone see the issue with fresh eyes. If the same argument resurfaces, stay grounded in your reasons. When siblings or children refuse to engage or criticize your timing, resist the urge to apologize for wanting order and peace in your home.

Remember, you're allowed to honor your boundaries even if others struggle with change. You can let go of things without letting go of love or respect for those around you. By staying compassionate but firm, using scripts that reflect empathy and clarity, you might just find that disagreements sting less... and sometimes even bring families closer as everyone learns to listen and adapt together.

The Pass-It-On Pile

Tell me there's anything more satisfying than watching a beloved possession land in the perfect new home. Well, that's the magic of the Pass-It-On Pile. At 45, I'm not *getting rid of stuff*; I'm curating a tiny boutique for people who will actually use it. This is about honoring what still has value and choosing its next chapter on purpose. Every house is packed with story-soaked bits: a scarf that still smells like laughter, a paperback hiding a pressed flower, the casserole dish that survived a decade of potlucks. When you gather them into a Pass-It-On Pile, you're not erasing your past, but sharing it, guilt-free, with someone who'll love it all over again.

Practicality goes hand in hand with sentiment here. I've found that labeling is the secret to keeping everything straight and making the process smoother for everyone. Sticky notes become tiny messengers, carrying the names of intended recipients and sometimes a little wink or a joke. Tags attached to handles, or even a master list on your phone, can prevent confusion when it's time to distribute everything. For special pieces, you can tuck in a handwritten note or even a short story, perhaps a favorite memory attached to that item. Maybe your sister gets the vase she always complimented, with a slip of paper inside sharing how it brightened every spring bouquet in your kitchen. Snapping a quick photo and texting it along with a message works beautifully, too.

Don't be afraid to make the act of passing things on festive. I once hosted a "family gifting night," complete with snacks and laughter, where everyone picked from the Pass-It-On Pile while I shared funny anecdotes about each item. For relatives or friends who live far away, sending surprise packages can turn an ordinary week into something special. Imagine your cousin opening a parcel to find that vintage brooch she admired year after year at Christmas —alongside a note recalling her playful attempts to sneak it into her suitcase. It's these small gestures that transform decluttering from a chore into an act of celebration. Grouping similar items (like recipe cards or costume jewelry) and making them little themed bundles can also be a hit. Sometimes, attaching a photo of the item in use (say, Aunt Helen wearing that hat at your wedding) brings back memories and adds personal flair.

Of course, not every gift will be met with tears of gratitude or wild excitement. Occasionally, you'll see polite smiles or get a "thanks, but no thanks." That's perfectly okay! It's important to release any expectation that every single item will find an ecstatic new owner. The satisfaction lies in the act of giving itself, knowing you've honored your history and extended connection, whether the object ends up cherished or quietly donated elsewhere. Remind yourself that it's the act of sharing, not the outcome, that creates legacy. You're planting seeds of memory and kindness, and how they're received is up to each person.

Sometimes, sharing becomes its own reward. There's unexpected delight when a neighbor lights up at receiving a book you loved or when a grandchild treasures an ornament you thought was forgotten. Even if something ends up in a thrift shop later, it may catch the eye of someone who needs exactly what you've let go. That possibility is worth celebrating in itself.

Organizing your Pass-It-On Pile can also be therapeutic, a visual reminder of progress and generosity blooming at the center of your efforts. You start to see your belongings as opportunities for connection and new stories rather than burdens. The process is simple, but meaningful: gather, label, share, and let go with intention and gratitude.

THE EMOTIONAL TERRAIN OF LETTING GO

Permission to Wait and Revisit

I once found myself clutching a porcelain cat from the 1980s, standing in the hallway, completely stuck. This cat wasn't particularly lovely, but it came from my Aunt June, who loved to collect oddities. As I stood there, frozen by a mix of guilt and nostalgia, I realized one truth: sometimes, you need a pause button for sorting through your past. That's when I discovered the power of the Guilt Box, and honestly, it changed everything.

The Guilt Box is your judgment-free zone, such as a physical bin, basket, or drawer dedicated to those "maybe" items that make you hesitate. When your heart can't let go, but your head knows you shouldn't keep everything, the Guilt Box steps in. It's not a dumping ground for indecision; it's a safe space where you give yourself permission to wait and revisit. If you feel torn over old letters, jewelry handed down from relatives, or gifts from friends that never quite fit your style, just place them in the Guilt Box instead of forcing a decision you're not ready to make. And just so we're clear, this isn't procrastination; it's self-compassion in action.

Indecision is human. Some days we feel bold enough to part with a stack of birthday cards; other days, just moving them out of sight is an achievement. There's no shame in honoring your own pace. To keep things gentle (and prevent the Guilt Box from turning into a permanent storage solution), I recommend labeling each item or the whole box with a revisit date, maybe three months ahead or after the next season changes. Write it on a bright sticky note: "Revisit on September 1" or "Check back after Thanksgiving." This creates a gentle boundary for yourself. You're not saying "no forever," just "not today."

You may find comfort in having a little script for self-talk when you set something aside. Try this phrase if guilt or uncertainty creeps in: "It's okay not to decide today. My feelings are valid." Say it softly or even out loud if it helps. Imagine you're talking to your best friend; compassion often comes easier when we address ourselves kindly. You're allowed to pause and revisit when you feel stronger or clearer. Sometimes, distance brings insight; sometimes, it brings relief.

Let me share Linda's story, which still makes me smile. Linda struggled for weeks with her late mother's costume jewelry. Every time she tried to sort it, she ended up tangled in memories and second-guessing herself. So, she started a Guilt Box and told herself she'd look again in six months. When she finally opened it months later, she felt a surprising sense of freedom. What once felt extremely precious or loaded with responsibility now looked like just a handful of trinkets. She was now ready to let most of it go, keeping one brooch and donating the rest without regret.

What typically ends up in the Guilt Box? From experience, old love letters are classic candidates, sometimes charming, sometimes cringeworthy. Jewelry from relatives is another frequent flyer, especially when you can't remember who wore what or if anyone in the family actually wants grandma's chunky turquoise necklace. Souvenirs from long-ago trips, postcards from former neighbors, or trinkets from work events that once seemed meaningful. Gifts from friends that never quite fit your taste or your lifestyle often find their way there, too. There's no rule about what belongs; if an item makes you waver, it qualifies.

The real magic of the Guilt Box is clarity over time. With distance, you often see objects for what they are, rather than what they represent emotionally. You may discover that you're ready to let go after all, or perhaps realize an item genuinely belongs in your life. Either outcome is progress. This small act of self-kindness can actually reduce anxiety and prevent impulsive decisions you might regret later. It's a fantastic way to avoid both the pain of forced goodbyes and the guilt of keeping things you no longer want.

Create Your Own Guilt Box

Take a moment now: find an empty bin, basket, or drawer and label it "Guilt Box." Place inside any items that leave you uncertain or tug at your heartstrings in a confusing way. Add a sticky note with your revisit date, and give yourself permission to pause. When the day comes, open the box in a calm moment (perhaps with a cup of tea) and check how your feelings have shifted.

You're not alone if you need time to decide what stays, what goes, and what simply needs rest for now. Trust that clarity grows when pressure is lifted.

The Guilt Box is wise stewardship of your own emotional landscape.

Letting Go Rituals

There's something deeply human about needing a little ceremony when saying goodbye, even if it's just to an old scarf, a chipped coffee mug, or that candle holder you swore matched *everything*. Letting go can feel final, and it's natural to hesitate, tangled in nostalgia, loyalty, or plain old stubborn love.

But rituals? Rituals have a way of flipping the script. They turn the moment from "loss" into something closer to affirmation. When you slow down and create a small goodbye ritual, you're not just releasing an object, you're honoring the memories, the version of yourself who once needed it, and the meaning it carried.

And these moments don't have to be reserved for life's grand finales. They're for the in-between times too. The ones where your hands hover just a second too long over the donate pile, and your brain pipes up with, *"But what if I need this again someday?"* That's when a tiny ceremony can help. Maybe you light a candle, close your eyes, and take a few steady breaths while remembering the role it played in your story. Some people whisper a quiet "thank you," while others prefer to share a quick memory aloud. ("This was the scarf I wore on my first trip to Paris," hits a lot differently than "This was the treadmill that became my laundry rack.")

Photos can also work wonders. Snap a picture, write a short farewell note, or tuck the memory into a journal or digital file. These acts create a bridge between past and present. You get to keep the memory, the story, the warm fuzzy feeling, all without needing the physical thing to weigh you down. Tidier home, lighter heart, and yes, still plenty of room for the good stuff.

Inviting others can also make the process lighter. I once hosted a "memory tea," gathering family around with tea and cinnamon buns. Each of us brought something to release, shared its story, and then sent our treasures on their way, whether to charity, a new home, or the recycling bin. It was both a celebration and a gentle therapy session, and deeply freeing. This can be done more simply, too: a friend on speakerphone as you clean a dresser, or asking a grandchild to help choose which books to pass on. There's strength and comfort in being witnessed as you say farewell.

Many women I've worked with have found these rituals restorative. Marsha told me that saying goodbye with a ritual made parting with her mother's scarf feel like a celebration, not a loss. She lit a candle, wore the scarf one last time, and shared her favorite memory before confidently donating it. Another friend sketched her childhood toys before donating them, creating "mementos without clutter." Even quick gestures help, for instance writing "thank you" on a sticky note before dropping off an old vase. You might discover that they can give surprising closure.

There are also rituals that blend Swedish tradition with personal touches. In Sweden, lighting candles is part of daily life and beautifully marks transitions. You might light a candle whenever you let go of something meaningful, honoring what's leaving and what's to come. Or perhaps you'll want to host a "farewell fika:" a coffee break to share item stories before they go, pouring coffee or tea, serving sweets, and taking turns spotlighting each object.

If you're unsure what feels right, experiment. The ritual doesn't need to be elaborate or photo-worthy; it just needs to resonate for *you*. You may find comfort in playing music as you pack up old letters, or in a small act such as leaving flowers by the donation box. What matters is pausing, reflecting, and honoring the transition instead of rushing through.

For those who want structure, here are a few ideas:

- Candle-lighting: Light a candle with the item, say goodbye or express thanks
- Memory sharing: Speak or write a story about the object

- Photo & note: Snap a photo and write a farewell note to keep
- Group ritual: Host a memory tea or coffee with friends/family
- Artful exit: Draw or paint the item as a keepsake

Letting go doesn't have to feel like some sterile, coldhearted purge. Honestly, it deserves better than that. Done right, it can be warm, intentional, and even joyful when you allow a little ritual into the mix. Think of it as pressing pause to honor both what was and who you're becoming: lighter, clearer, and more ready than ever for whatever comes next.

The Memory Lane Walk

The process of letting go isn't always about cutting ties. In fact, it often turns out to be about honoring the path you've walked and the memories you've collected along the way.

I've found that sorting through the belongings of a well-lived life is less about the objects themselves and more about the stories they hold. You might pick up a faded theater program and find yourself transported back to opening night, the thrill of applause, the scent of old velvet seats. Those moments deserve a pause, a little space to breathe before you decide whether to keep or release. That's where the Memory Lane Walk comes in. An intentional, unhurried stroll through your things, designed not to rush decisions, but to let each story step forward and be recognized.

Set aside a quiet hour, maybe on a Sunday afternoon when the house feels calm and there's no pressure to finish. I like to settle in with a cup of coffee or tea, perhaps with soft music in the background, to signal that this isn't a chore but a celebration of memory. As you pick up each item, allow yourself to ask: Where did this come from? Who was there with me? What did it mean to me back then? Sometimes, an answer comes quickly. A photograph might bring back laughter shared on a family vacation, or a chipped salad bowl might remind you of long conversations at the kitchen table. Other times, memories are more elusive, hiding behind years and dust, but even then, the act of asking gives value to your experience.

Consider inviting someone else into the Memory Lane Walk. Sometimes, sorting is richer when shared. A daughter might remember wearing your old scarf to her first job interview, or a friend might remind you of the wild camping trip where you both swore never to eat canned beans again. When you let others chime in, you'll find that objects hold different meanings for everyone. Invite your child or a close friend to sit with you as you reminisce. Let them handle an item and share what it means to them. You may discover new stories or realize that something you're ready to part with is treasured by someone else. This act of shared remembering can turn a potentially challenging task into a source of connection and laughter.

Now, listen: I know how difficult it can be to let go, especially following a sentimental stroll down memory lane. That's why recording these stories ensures they last, even if the object does not. Record a quick voice memo on your phone (or go delightfully retro with a tape recorder): tell how your wedding ring was chosen, or capture your child's giggle while you describe the first pie you baked in that battle-scarred tin. Prefer writing? Attach "memory tags" to items heading to new homes—a short note that preserves their significance for the next person. Slip a card inside a cookbook: "Every Christmas we made the cinnamon rolls on page 67. The flour always ended up on the dog." Imagine someone discovering that tucked-away note (a small, human spark passed forward) while you enjoy the lightness of a home that holds stories, not just stuff.

Not every memory needs to be grand or profound. Sometimes, it's a single moment: the sweater you wore on your first date after your divorce, an ornament from a friend who moved away, a keychain from a job you loved (or hated). These small recollections are threads in the fabric of your life. Write them down if you wish, or snap a photo that captures both the object and its story scribbled on an index card beside it. If an item feels like it deserves its own chapter in your family's narrative, consider starting a "legacy notebook," a place where these stories can live on beyond their physical trappings.

Reflection doesn't have to slow progress; in truth, it often accelerates it. Once an object's story is voiced or written down, many women find it easier to let go. **The fear of losing the memory fades because it's been preserved in another form.** I've seen daughters cherish their mother's stories more than her china set; I've seen sons laugh over their father's tales of army days rather than needing every badge or medal.

If you want a little help getting started, try asking yourself:

What season of life does this object remind me of?

Would someone else be glad to know this story if I shared it?

Does holding this item bring comfort, gratitude, or just confusion?

If you feel moved by something as you sort (a song lyric scribbled on an envelope or a pressed flower from an old diary) pause and honor it with words before moving along.

Treating your belongings as chapters in your story changes everything about Swedish death cleaning. No longer is it just about clearing space; it becomes an act of honoring your past and sharing it with those around you, or even strangers who might find joy in what you release. Whether through spoken tales, written notes, or simple moments of remembrance, each step along Memory Lane will allow you to move forward with clarity and heart.

When Sentimental Items Feel Impossible

Few things feel as impossible as sorting through objects that seem to pulse with memory. You're not alone if you've ever found yourself staring at your wedding dress, unable to move it from its box, or holding your child's first shoes with a lump in your throat. The watch that once belonged to your late partner, the necklace your mother gave you for your thirtieth birthday, the stack of letters from a friend who moved away. So much more than things, these are time capsules, small containers for love, loss, and laughter. The pain of parting with them can feel sharp, sometimes even unfair. If you've ever caught yourself thinking, "How could I possibly let this go?" please know, this is universal. The struggle is real and it's valid.

To make the process gentler, break it down into slow, deliberate steps. Start by removing the item from your daily line of sight and placing it somewhere safe, like a shelf, a box in your closet, a drawer that's out of regular reach. This creates emotional distance and lets your mind rest, even if only for a few days. Once the object is relocated, allow yourself to sit with the feelings that bubble up. Maybe the ache comes right away; maybe it sneaks up later in the week. Journaling about it or talking with a trusted friend can help you untangle what's sorrow, what's nostalgia, and what's simply habit. You might write, "I remember dancing in these shoes at my wedding," or say to a friend, "I feel guilty even thinking about giving this up." Processing aloud or on paper gives shape to emotions that otherwise swirl in silence.

When you feel ready, contemplate your next move: keep, donate, gift, or repurpose. Keeping is always an option; no rule says you must let go just because you're sorting. If you decide to donate or gift, do so with intention. Sometimes knowing an object will be loved by someone else eases the ache. Gifting a ring to a niece or passing down a beloved quilt can transform grief into pride. If letting go feels too harsh, repurposing can offer a soft landing. That shirt from your late husband? It might become a memory pillow, a tangible comfort that still carries his warmth. Old letters and photographs can be digitized, scanned to preserve every word and image without taking up space in drawers. You could even frame a single letter or create a small photo album of the most meaningful moments.

If the idea of parting still stings, creative alternatives abound. I've heard from women who transformed wedding gowns into christening blankets for grandchildren or stitched together baby clothes into quilts. One friend took pieces from family linens and made sachets for each daughter, every gift infused with the scent and texture of family history. Digitizing mementos has become easier than ever, so scan those love letters and photograph treasured objects so you can revisit them without cluttering your shelves.

Family decisions are rarely simple. When loved ones are involved, especially when dividing heirlooms or deciding what stays in the family, it helps to use scripts that invite understanding rather than conflict. You might say, "It's okay to love the memory, not the object." Or for those moments when sharing feels right: "Passing this quilt along to my niece means our family story continues." These words will help shift focus from guilt or obligation to shared meaning and joy.

Reassuring self-talk is powerful during these times of transition.

Remind yourself:

Letting go doesn't erase the love I felt.

It's normal to have mixed feelings. I'm honoring what matters.

I want this piece to bring happiness to someone else now.

Sometimes the answer is simply to wait and see how your feelings shift with time and space. But if today is the day you're ready to decide, remember that **sentiment lives in the *stories*** attached to objects.

Whenever you feel overwhelmed by the weight of sentimentality, break things down to one small step at a time. Remove the item. Sit with your feelings. Decide what comes next, whether it's keeping, sharing, transforming, or simply pausing once more. Every decision made with care becomes an act of self-respect and a tribute to your lived experience.

Journaling Prompts for Emotional Release

There's something quietly healing about sitting down with a pen and a blank page. No audience. No judgment. Just you, your thoughts, and maybe the comforting sound of a kettle boiling in the background. When we're struggling to let go of objects, memories, or the guilt tangled up in both, journaling can be the pressure valve that keeps us from imploding.

Forget perfect grammar or channeling your inner Shakespeare. Even scribbled bullet points, half-sentences, or a dramatic "UGH, WHY IS THIS SO HARD" can do wonders. Putting thoughts on paper has a way of untangling the emotional knots, softening sharp edges, and reminding us that most "immovable walls" are really just stacks of swirling worries in disguise. In the end, reading our own words becomes like a mirror to our inner world, offering nonjudgmental reflection, which can lead to closure and self-compassion.

If staring at the page makes you feel like you've been thrown into a high school essay exam, don't panic. Prompts are your trusty lifeboat. Use them as starting points, and let the words tumble out however they need to.

Prompts to Try:

- *What am I most afraid to let go of, and why?*
- *What do I fear will happen if I let this go? Is this fear realistic?*
- *What possessions hold the most emotional weight for me right now?*
- *If I could speak to or thank the person who gave me this item, what would I say?*
- *If I could thank the item itself for its role in my life, what would I say?*
- *Am I holding onto this for myself, or for someone else's expectations?*
- *Which objects would I want to explain the story behind?*
- *Does keeping this support the woman I am today, or the woman I used to be?*
- *What story have I attached to this object, and is it still true?*
- *Who could benefit from receiving this item now?*
- *What space, physically or emotionally, would open up for me if I let this go?*
- *How do I hope my loved ones feel when they remember me?*
- *How would I feel if my loved ones had to sort through this after I'm gone?*

The style you use is up to you. Some prefer writing letters, like addressing a note to a loved one, alive or gone, as if speaking across time. Others like lists; a simple "things I'm ready to release" builds momentum and marks progress. Stream-of-consciousness writing lets thoughts spill out unfiltered, sometimes revealing hidden patterns. Or try "memory snapshots," jotting down a moment tied to an object, then leaving that memory on the page. These entries are for your eyes only, unless you wish to share them.

Writing usually brings unexpected comfort and understanding. Use any prompt that resonates, letting your writing follow your feelings. And if nothing comes to mind, simply writing "I don't know what to write" can break the block and open the door to something deeper.

Journaling doesn't require fancy supplies; a plain notebook or a digital document works fine. Use whatever feels natural and accessible. Consider setting aside ten minutes each morning or evening to journal, or simply write when strong emotions arise during decluttering. Some days you'll write pages, other days only a sentence or two, but honesty matters more than quantity.

From my own experience and from others', journaling often brings closure that objects alone cannot. Sometimes after writing, letting go becomes easier; other times, journaling affirms that holding on has meaning right now. Both outcomes are valid and help move you toward peace.

Finally, remember that your journal is just for you, so no need for performance or perfection. Turning emotions into words brings order, even momentarily, to chaos. Where clutter once felt overwhelming, journaling sorts out your feelings, one thought at a time, making way for self-compassion and the courage you need to continue your Swedish death cleaning journey on your own terms.

Building Emotional Resilience

What if I regret it?

Regret often shadows big decisions, especially when you're sorting through years of sentimental items. It's human to worry about missing something once it's gone. The fear of letting go and then regretting it can easily stall your progress. I've felt it too. Each item seems to whisper, "What if you need me again?" Sometimes it's nostalgia, sometimes anxiety, or just the nagging "what if." You may fret about discarding something that one day might matter, or worry a family member will look for something you no longer have.

All of this is completely normal.

Instead of letting these worries freeze you, try viewing regret as a natural part of the process, not a punishment for making a decision. I keep a "Keepsakes Set Free" photo folder on my phone. Simply seeing these images reassures me, though I rarely look back at them. Another strategy is to make a "regret safety net" list: choose a handful of items you're not ready to part with, no explanation needed. Give yourself permission to keep these now and revisit your decision later.

If second-guessing strikes, speak to yourself with kindness. Remind yourself, "I made the best choice with the information and emotions I had then." This gentle affirmation helps ease the pressure of perfection and highlights that your decisions are good enough for who you are now. I also remind myself, "**My memories are not held in objects, but in my heart.**" The value in my grandmother's teacup, for example, was in the memories it represented—not in the porcelain.

True regret after mindful decluttering is rare, despite late-night worries. Most women who've undergone Swedish death cleaning report relief more than remorse. Studies and experiences show that intentional decluttering almost never leads to lasting sorrow. The process of deciding allows for control and clarity, while regret tends to be fleeting.

If the fear of letting go persists, try this exercise: Make two lists. First, write items you fear you'll regret losing. Second, jot down what you've already donated or tossed in the past year. You'll likely find that you rarely regret what you've already parted with. This perspective helps you trust your decisions. And if an item keeps popping into your mind after it's gone, consider what it symbolized, for example comfort, security, connection. Often, these needs can be addressed in new ways, apart from the object itself.

Sometimes, a small pang of regret might appear, perhaps when you see an old photo or hear a story about something you parted with. In those moments, remind yourself that choosing to let go was an act of self-care. Connect with friends or family who've gone through similar experiences, as their stories usually show that lasting regret is rare.

Emotional resilience doesn't imply never feeling sad or nostalgic, but accepting those feelings and knowing they pass. Nostalgia is natural; it means you cared. But it's equally valid to **prioritize your peace and space** in the present, rather than live in fear of possible regrets. Each thoughtful decision you make is a sign of growing self-trust, which will help you worry less about uncertain futures.

Reflection Prompts to Build Emotional Resilience

- **When nostalgia hits:** What memory is attached to this item, and can I honor that memory in a different way (a photo, a journal entry, a story shared with loved ones)?
- **When fear of regret creeps in:** What's the *worst-case scenario* if I let this go? And if that happened, could I still handle it? (Spoiler: yes, you could.)
- **When guilt shows up:** Am I holding onto this out of love, or out of obligation? Whose peace matters here, mine, or the person who gave it to me years ago?

- **When you need a pep talk:** What do I gain (in space, peace, or freedom) by letting this go?

Remember: fearing regret is natural, but it doesn't have to control you. Keep moving forward by doing the work that lightens both your heart and your home, and use your new tools and self-compassion to carry you through the process. Emotional resilience is your Swedish death cleaning superpower.

SUSTAINING SIMPLICITY

By now, you've probably realized that Swedish death cleaning isn't a single, dramatic purge; it's a sustainable practice that adapts as your life changes, much like tending a perennial garden. After several final closet cleanouts and watching outgrown souvenirs resurface, I learned that lasting simplicity requires ongoing attention. Our needs and lives evolve, so our approach to decluttering should too.

To fully grasp this principle, I like to think of Swedish death cleaning as a gentle, recurring ritual synchronized with the year's natural rhythms. Rather than tackling huge projects once in a while, I create a personalized calendar for small, focused actions every month or season. This approach borrows from Scandinavian traditions of syncing routines to nature, like the springtime urge to air out homes and reassess what's hiding in neglected corners.

Getting practical, you don't need fancy planners to do this. Just use a basic wall calendar, notebook, or digital file, whatever feels easiest. Divide your home into sensible zones or categories. Each month or quarter, target one area without pressure to do everything at once. In January, you might choose to focus on paperwork, clearing out old files and updating essential records. April, as you bring out lighter spring clothes, means revisiting your wardrobe to donate what no longer fits. October can be for holiday decorations, edited before festivities begin so you keep only what's meaningful. This pacing builds steady progress and keeps any single task from feeling overwhelming.

Here's an example of a Swedish Death Cleaning Calendar. Use it as-is or adapt based on your circumstances. Print it, hang it, or save it where you'll see it often. Some months will be light, like weeding out expired spices. Others, such as organizing the garage, may be more involved, so schedule those for times when you have extra help or energy.

Swedish Death Cleaning Calendar

Month	Focus Area	Example Task
January	Paperwork	Shred old files, update records
February	Kitchen	Clear expired foods, gadgets
March	Living Room	Pare down decor, books
April	Wardrobe	Try on clothes, donate unused
May	Outdoor Spaces	Sort garden tools, patio items
June	Photos	Organize albums, digitize prints
July	Bathroom	Toss expired products
August	Kids' Stuff	Pass on toys, artwork
September	Storage Areas	Edit ornaments, donate excess
October	Holiday Decor	Document stories, pass on items
December	Review & Reflect	Celebrate wins, set new goals

Feel free to swap out categories to fit your lifestyle: moving, new family members, or big life changes all call for flexible priorities. The point is to personalize your calendar so it suits both your practical needs and your emotional life.

Life rarely follows a neat schedule, so embrace flexibility. If energy dips or family demands arise, adjust your calendar and don't feel guilty for pausing or scaling back. Some seasons are for rest as much as sorting; small wins are successes too. Use the calendar as an extra tool for self-care and compassion, rather than just organization.

The check-ins are a regular review that will help keep your legacy goals current. What's important now may not be next year, and that's healthy. The calendar should evolve with you, staying flexible and affirming rather than rigid.

This consistent, cyclical approach means you will avoid dramatic, stressful cleanouts and the anxiety of leaving a mess for others. You'll worry less about hidden clutter and feel more comfortable welcoming guests or hosting gatherings, knowing your home is in step with your life.

The Declutter Buddy System

If you've been avoiding the guest room like it's a haunted closet, hi—same. Decluttering can feel like hacking through a jungle of feelings, dust bunnies, and sentimental items and obligations. The secret is that you don't have to do it solo. Social support fundamentally changes the process. Having a declutter buddy who encourages you, nudges you along, and even laughs with you at forgotten oddities often spells the difference between endless procrastination and real progress.

Research (and real-life experience) shows that accountability leads to lasting results. The way a workout friend gets you lacing shoes at 6 a.m., a Declutter Buddy keeps you honest when your energy tanks or a keep/donate decision gets squirmy. They set a 10-minute timer, hand you the donation bag, and ask the magic question: "Does this earn space in your future?" Honestly, most people get more done in one afternoon with encouragement than in three months of solo sighing. Sometimes, merely sharing your plan jump-starts action; other times, knowing someone will ask, "Did those old VHS tapes finally leave?" keeps you honest.

Picking a clutter-buddy isn't about finding someone with a label maker obsession or a Pinterest-perfect home. It's about trust. You want the kind of person who won't judge you for crying over a chipped bowl from 1997. Your person might be your sister who lives two time zones away, the neighbor who alphabetizes her spice rack for fun, or a fellow declutterer from an online group who just *gets it.*

Choose someone patient and kind, but also brave enough to tell you when that "vintage" candle holder is really just a dust collector. You want a cheerleader who celebrates your tiniest wins (like finally letting go of those jeans that haven't fit since 2004) but who also knows when to lovingly nudge you forward.

And here's the secret bonus: most people will be thrilled by not having to tackle their own chaos alone. They'll jump at the chance to join you, armed with coffee, moral support, and maybe a few judgment-free laughs along the way.

Alright. So, once you've chosen your partner, set some basic ground rules. Decide how often you'll check in; every Sunday, twice a month, whatever works. Will you text updates? Share photos? Video chat? Decide together. Clear expectations prevent misunderstandings. Agree on your preferred style of encouragement, as some like gentle nudges, others thrive on enthusiastic reminders. If one of you feels stuck, brainstorm together or just listen without judgment. The goal is mutual support, not criticism.

Make it fun to stay engaged: schedule "declutter and coffee" FaceTime dates, tackle a small task while chatting, or set mini-challenges (who can fill a donate box first?). Celebrate milestones with small rewards like a treat, flowers, or a chore-free afternoon. Some people exchange before-and-after photos weekly, turning updates into mini-pep rallies. Playful competition really helps keep things light and connected.

Of course, real life can interrupt the best-laid plans. Schedules may not always align, motivation may wane, or goals may shift. If enthusiasm lags or one of you drifts away for a bit, try a gentle reset: "Missed our updates! Want to pick a new day or try a smaller goal?" You can even make things official with a simple buddy contract where you write down your goals, sign your names, or keep a shared journal documenting victories and funny moments. This can make accountability memorable and meaningful.

If you and your buddy have different energy levels or shifting priorities, talk openly about what's working. Adjust your pace or check-in style. Maybe shorter updates suit you both better, or switching from weekly to monthly works best. Flexibility is key; the priority is kindness and encouragement.

Many women find online groups helpful if local support isn't available. Posting progress, exchanging tips, or sharing struggles in a private forum creates camaraderie without pressure. You might discover new ideas or simply commiserate about letting go of mismatched mugs.

Accountability shouldn't feel like a burden. It can spark momentum when motivation fades and provide comfort knowing you're not in this alone. Whether your buddy is next door or on the other side of the world, what matters most is lifting each other up, celebrating every bit of progress, and laughing together through even the messiest moments.

Progress Trackers to Map Your Success

Watching your progress unfold can be motivating and surprisingly satisfying. There's real magic in seeing cluttered spaces transform, one small area at a time, into places you want to open.

For the women who get an almost physical thrill from ticking a box or scratching through a to-do list (you know who you are), visual tools can mean the difference between feeling stuck and feeling accomplished. Even if you don't consider yourself a visual learner, you'll likely notice a boost in motivation once you start tracking what you've accomplished. It becomes easier to keep going, even on days when you'd rather binge a True Crime series than deal with the hallway closet.

I recommend using a wall chart on your fridge or inside a closet door, a simple grid listing every room or category you want to tackle. Each time you finish a task, add a sticker, stamp, or check mark. As the visual proof builds, the work starts to feel achievable, a series of small victories instead of one big, impossible job. If you love color-coding, try assigning shades to each project: blue for the kitchen, yellow for paperwork, green for keepsakes. Watching a rainbow grow on your chart becomes its own reward.

Before-and-after photos are also powerful. Snap a quick "before" picture of a chaotic drawer or closet, and then take an "after" shot from the same angle. The contrast is often remarkable and will motivate you to keep going, even for small changes. These photos are a wonderful proof of progress.

If you're a digital diva or just someone who's allergic to paper clutter (ironic, I know), whip up an online album or slideshow to track your Swedish Death Cleaning adventures. Whether you keep it private or share it with your ride-or-die friends, seeing your "before and afters" pile up feels *ridiculously* satisfying. Go ahead and caption them with flair: *"Goodbye, seven identical spatulas—may you rest in utensil heaven."* I also like to add notes about how the space feels now versus before. Soon enough, you'll have your own little museum of progress, a memory book of calm spaces and liberated shelves.

And if you're the type who gets heart-fluttery over color-coded systems and checklists (hi, kindred spirit), you're going to adore the templates in the Resource Toolkit at the back of this book. Some are neat little grids; others are dreamy open-ended maps where you can doodle your plans like the creative genius you are. The trick is to keep your milestones visible. Hang your tracker on the fridge, tuck it into your planner, or stick it right where you drink your morning coffee so you can bask in your own brilliance daily. Big win or baby step, celebrate it. Seriously, throw confetti. You've earned it.

Tips for Making Your Progress Photos Pop

- For "before" shots, capture the space as it is, without tidying it up first. Honest photos show real change. For "afters," use natural light and focus on clear, tidy surfaces. You're not aiming for magazine perfection, just authentic transformation you'll be proud to see every day.

- If you hit a discouraging patch mid-project, glance back at your chart, map, or album. Remember everything you've already accomplished. Progress won't always be rapid; some weeks blaze by, others crawl. That's normal. The point is to see your commitment taking visible shape.

- Celebrate small wins to keep momentum alive. Whether it's a chart peppered with gold stars, a "before-and-after" photo album, or the smile on your daughter's face as she applies a sticker, visual trackers are precious reminders that every step forward matters and every bit of effort deserves recognition.

Building Rituals for Annual Mini Death Cleanings

Rituals can transform even the most tedious tasks into moments you actually look forward to. Swedish death cleaning thrives on this concept: small, joyful ceremonies that breathe new life into what might otherwise feel like a chore. Imagine the difference between tackling the pantry in silence versus turning it into a spring tradition, complete with cinnamon buns, laughter, and a favorite playlist humming in the background. When you treat decluttering as an annual ritual, it blends naturally into your year, becoming as normal as baking a cake for someone's birthday or lighting candles during winter's darkness.

Some of the most successful mini death cleanings I've seen happen around meaningful dates. You might decide that every birthday is your day to sort a single drawer, letting go of what you no longer need while making space for new chapters. Or perhaps New Year's Day becomes your moment to choose one area and give it a fresh start along with your resolutions. Seasonal changes also lend themselves beautifully to this rhythm: as crocuses poke up in March or leaves begin to fall in October, pause and gently reassess a part of your home that has quietly gathered excess.

These rituals don't have to be grand. In fact, the charm lies in their simplicity and in the anticipation they build year after year. For instance, on the first Saturday of spring, I always gather my family and declare it "Pantry Renewal Day." We open each shelf, toss expired cans, wipe surfaces, and then reward ourselves with homemade cinnamon buns (store-bought are also perfectly acceptable—no one is grading your authenticity). We light a candle on the kitchen table as we work and play a folk playlist in the background, or sometimes (if I'm feeling nostalgic), some classic ABBA to add sparkle to even the dustiest corners.

If you prefer solo decluttering, it's just as easy to make it a personal ritual. Brew a strong cup of coffee, set a timer for 30 minutes, and focus your energy on one small area. When the timer buzzes, don't rush into another task. Treat yourself to fika: a coffee break with something sweet. Place fresh flowers on the counter as a visible signal of your accomplishment. Savor the satisfaction of a job well done and let that feeling linger.

Add Swedish touches wherever possible for an extra layer of delight. Bake cardamom buns or saffron bread as a post-cleaning treat—your home will smell incredible and you'll have something delicious to share. Place small candles on windowsills or tables to create warmth. Even a simple string of fairy lights can add coziness to an ordinary evening spent sorting photos or clearing drawers.

Rituals shine brightest when they include different generations. Invite children and grandchildren to join, giving them simple jobs like sorting old toys or choosing books to donate together. Children often bring an honest perspective and an infectious sense of fun to the process. With their help, decluttering becomes less about loss and more about passing along both memories and practical wisdom. They'll remember these moments long after the toys have found new homes.

Moreover, passing down these rituals builds family legacy beyond objects. Perhaps your daughter will carry on "Letting Go Night" with her own children someday, or your grandson will remember baking buns after helping you clear out the pantry each spring. The ritual itself can become a cherished tradition, one that marks time, strengthens bonds, and teaches that homes are living spaces meant for growth, not storage.

The Gentle Art of Living Lightly: Your Legacy of Love

There may come a day when you open your closet, kitchen, or even that infamous junk drawer and find only what you truly need or cherish. No silent reproach from the pile of untouched gadgets or a sweater you swore you'd wear again someday. This is what living lightly feels like; space for your favorite memories, room to breathe, and a home that celebrates the present rather than clings to the past. Simplicity doesn't mean stripping life bare or living in stark minimalism, but making room for what matters most: laughter echoing in the hallway, a special mug for your morning coffee, or the comfort of knowing you have just enough and not a bit more than you can love or use.

Choosing intention over accumulation isn't a one-time decision; it's a gentle habit that grows stronger with daily practice. Alongside the practical steps we've already explored, add in a weekly gratitude reflection for the space you've gained. Maybe it's a cleared shelf where a favorite vase can shine, or the empty corner that now fits a cozy chair for reading. Take a moment each week to notice these pockets of openness. Say thank you—to yourself, for having the courage to let go, and to your home, for holding only what serves you now.

Keep in my mind that Swedish death cleaning is not a finish line to cross. It's a living act of care for yourself, your family, and those who will walk through your home after you. As your needs shift and seasons change, so will your relationship with your belongings. Every item released represents a story shared with someone else, a weight lifted from your own shoulders, and often a joy multiplied as your things find new life in other hands. Legacy is built moment by moment, choice by choice, not just in what you keep but also in what you courageously release.

There will be days when the process feels easy, almost second nature. Other times, nostalgia or uncertainty may slow you down. This is normal for anyone who has lived a rich and layered life. On tough days, forgive yourself for any stumbles or pauses along the way.

Progress is never measured by perfection, but by your willingness to return again and again to the question:

Does this still serve me?

If not, can I let it go with love?

You are writing your legacy every day, with every item kept or released, every story told or passed on. The beauty of this process is that it's yours alone; no one else can define what "just enough" means for you. Take pride in the order you create, however small.

Simplicity gives us room for more joy, deeper relationships, and clearer thinking. The freedom we create in our home ripples outward into our family and community. There's no need for grand gestures. Living lightly becomes second nature when intention guides our choices.

In the end, Swedish death cleaning is an evolving act of love. It's love for yourself (because you deserve a calm, uncluttered space) and love for the people who'll one day sort through your things (and silently thank you for not keeping every take-out menu from 1998). This process isn't about living with less, but making room for more—the good kind of more.

More laughter.

More connection.

> More breathing space.

And every time you decide to let something go, you're really saying, "I'm choosing peace over chaos today." So celebrate your progress, forgive the messy days, and keep your sense of humor handy. Simplicity is your love language now; first for you, and then for everyone lucky enough to orbit your beautifully decluttered world.

THE GENTLE ART OF BEGINNING AGAIN

Here we are, at the end of a journey that started not with a grand gesture, but perhaps with a sheepish glance at a crowded attic, a sigh over a crammed closet, or the discovery of three fondue sets you don't remember acquiring.

If you're reading this, you've allowed yourself to wonder: Is there a gentler way to live with (and let go of) the things that fill our homes and hearts?

I hope you now see that the answer is a resounding *yes*.

But this journey wasn't really about stuff, was it? It never is. Sure, there were boxes, donation bags, and a few emotional landmines tucked between the Christmas ornaments and your old jeans, but what you really did was *shift*. You rewrote what "enough" means. You made peace with your past and cleared space for your future. That's no small thing.

Every item you let go of whispered, *"Thank you, I've done my job."* Every space you cleared became a little declaration of independence. And every laugh, sigh, and sentimental pause along the way became proof that you're human; gloriously, imperfectly human.

Maybe, along the way, you've discovered the magic in the mundane. The way a clean counter can feel like a deep breath, the way "just enough" can feel like abundance. You've perhaps contemplated rituals of release, added humor to hard moments, and maybe even discovered that cinnamon buns make excellent post-decluttering rewards (science would back me on this, I'm sure).

And here's the most beautiful part: you're not done. This isn't a journey that ends when you close this book. It's the kind that quietly seeps into your mornings and weekends, shaping how you choose, how you live, and how you feel in your own space. Maybe it's a candle flickering while you sort through old photos. Maybe it's a legacy moment when you tell your daughter why that necklace means so much. It's the gentle reminder that simplicity isn't a finish line, but a way of life.

So, if tomorrow gets messy again (because it will), don't panic. Make yourself a cup of tea. Put on some music. Pick one drawer. One shelf. One small act of reclaiming your space. Progress is cumulative, and peace is contagious.

And when you look around, I hope you see more than tidy shelves. I hope you see a woman who decided to live intentionally.

A woman who swapped guilt for grace.

A woman who turned "too much" into "just right."

Because that's the real legacy. Not the heirlooms, not the labels, not the perfectly folded towels. It's the calm you created, the laughter you shared, and the clarity you left behind.

So go ahead and light the candle, open the window, and breathe in the Scandinavian wisdom of *lagom är bäst* — just enough is best.

BONUS: SWEDISH DEATH CLEANING TOOLKIT

Welcome to your *lagom*-inspired toolkit, that magical Swedish balance between too much and too little.

This is your gentle, color-coded, checklist-happy companion for turning all that beautiful theory into satisfying action. It is your GPS through the forest of clutter: calm voice, no judgment, minimal recalculating.

So, pour yourself a cup of something warm (Swedes insist), and let's set up your system.

THE MINDFUL ART OF SWEDISH DEATH CLEANING

1. COLOR CODED CLARITY SYSTEM

COLOR CODED CLARITY SYSTEM

Color makes everything better... even paperwork and sock drawers. Use soft pastel markers or washi tape to visually sort your progress and prevent the dreaded "what did I mean by this box?" moment later.

COLOR	MEANING	USE IT FOR
Sage Green	Keep	Items that serve your current life or spark calm joy.
Dusty Rose	Gift/Pass On	Beloved items you want to rehome with intention.
Soft Sky Blue	Donate	Gently used pieces ready for a new chapter.
Linen Beige	Recycle/Dispose	Broken, expired, or guilt-inducing clutter.
Gold Highlight	Legacy Treasures	The heirlooms and memory-rich gems to document and share.

2. 🎒 THE MASTER CHECKLIST

Here's to transitioning from chaos to calm. No frantic cleaning montages here, just steady, satisfying progress.

Step 1: Prep & Plan 📋

- Choose one small area.
- Gather supplies: boxes, labels, tea.
- Set your *Fika Timer*.

Step 2: Sort & Simplify 🧺

- Use your color codes.
- Take "before" photos.
- Sort items into *Keep, Gift, Donate, Recycle, Legacy*.

Step 3: Reflect & Record 📝

- Write short notes in your *Heritage Journal* for any meaningful items.
- Snap photos of sentimental items you're letting go of.
- Add stories or notes to your *Legacy Inventory Grid*.

Step 4: Release & Celebrate

- Deliver donations or gifts.
- Take a *Fika Break*.
- Light a candle for closure and gratitude.

3. 📋 LEGACY INVENTORY GRID

Use this mini-table (print or recreate in your journal) to capture what really matters: the stories, not just the stuff.

BONUS: SWEDISH DEATH CLEANING TOOLKIT

Legacy Inventory Grid

Item Description	Story / Memory	Pass-It-On Plan (Who / When / How)	Photo
Gold locket	Gift from Aunt Evelyn, worn on my wedding day	For Anna on her 21st birthday	
China teapot	Grandma's Sunday tea tradition	Give to Sophie at family reunion	
Hand-stitched quilt	Sewn with Mom during winter 1989	Pass to Claire when she moves	

Hint: Don't overthink it. One sentence per item is enough to carry generations of meaning.

THE MINDFUL ART OF SWEDISH DEATH CLEANING

4. 🍄 CLUTTER HOTSPOT MAP

Draw a quick sketch of your home.

Mark each spot that makes you sigh with a soft "X": those are your hotspots. Then, color the Xs by intensity:

🌸 Light Pink: manageable clutter (junk drawer).

🌿 Green: emotionally loaded zones (photos, heirlooms).

☁ Blue: big projects (garage, attic, storage).

Each time you tackle one, cross it off and reward yourself with something small like a walk, a slice of cake, or five guilt-free minutes of scrolling Scandinavian cabin interiors .

5. ⏰ THE 10-MINUTE DECLUTTER GRID

Meet your new döstädning sidekick: a cute little grid that turns "ugh, clutter" into a 10-minute mic drop.

Pick a box, hit the timer, do the tiny task, then bask in that lighter/free/virtuous/calm glow like you just benched emotional baggage. The mini rewards? Totally on purpose, because a coffee refill and a blast of ABBA are scientifically proven* to make you unstoppable.

So start anywhere, keep it easy, and watch these micro-wins snowball into a home that finally feels like you. (*By me. I'm the scientist.)

THE MINDFUL ART OF SWEDISH DEATH CLEANING

LOCATION	MINI TASK	MOOD AFTER	REWARD
(drawer)	Toss dead batteries, sort utensils	Lighter	Coffee refill
(car)	Remove ancient receipts	Free!	Roll down windows, blast ABBA
(jar)	Toss expired skincare	Virtuous	Apply that fancy serum
(hanger)	One hanger section only	Calm	10 minutes of TikTok in peace

Pick one box. Set a timer. Done in 10.

6. ☕ THE FIKA FORMULA

Decluttering is absolutely not punishment. In fact, it's a tremendous act of love... and that means mandatory breaks.

How to Fika Like a Pro:

1. Brew something delicious.
2. Light a candle or open a window.
3. Sit down and *do nothing* productive for 15 minutes.
4. Bonus points if a cat joins you.

Repeat after every completed checklist, because joy and progress pair beautifully with caffeine and a pastry.

7. THE LOVING LEGACY MAP

Create your personal *Legacy Map*, a visual reflection of what matters most.

Draw circles for:

- **Family & Friends** (connections)
- **Values** (what you stand for)
- **Stories** (moments you want remembered)
- **Treasures** (objects worth keeping)

Connect them with dotted lines, and you'll start seeing that your *true legacy* isn't in things at all, but in relationships, laughter, and love.

❉ FINAL NOTE

Swedish death cleaning is about filling your life with space, meaning, and peace.

This toolkit isn't a rulebook, it's a companion; equal parts checklist, cheerleader, and cozy Scandinavian coffee break.

So please, go slow. Breathe deep. Laugh often.

And when in doubt, remember: if it doesn't serve your life today, or tell a story worth passing on, it's okay to let it go.

POSTSCRIPT

Hello, Lovely Keeper of Stories,

Look at you, crossing the finish line with grace, grit, and probably a suspiciously full *miscellaneous* drawer.

When I first sat down to draft this book, I had in mind women just like you; women who are done apologizing for having a life's worth of memories. Women who are ready to keep the best, pass on the rest, and breathe easier in a home that feels like calm. Less clutter. More clarity. Fewer "where did I put my reading glasses?" scavenger hunts.

My hope is that you're leaving these pages with more than a tidy linen closet and a labeled photo box. I hope you've found a deeper trust in your choices, kinder boundaries with your stuff, and a softer rhythm to your days; one where a candlelit corner and a cup of coffee count as a win.

If this book helped you, would you take a minute to **leave a kind review on Amazon**? Your words help other women find

POSTSCRIPT

their way to a calmer home and a clearer heart. (Side effects may include better sleep, fewer tripping hazards, and the smug joy of opening a drawer that *actually* closes.)

Sending you courage, coziness, and beautifully labeled boxes.

— *Linnea Maren Bergman*

JOIN OUR TRIBE

The Mindful Art of Swedish Death Cleaning for Women Over 50

A Gentle Scandinavian Method to Declutter, Downsize, Organize, and Leave a Loving Legacy

A TES Publication © Copyright 2025 by Linnea M. Bergman - All rights reserved

BIBLIOGRAPHY

- *Swedish death cleaning* https://en.wikipedia.org/wiki/Swedish_death_cleaning
- *The Gentle Art of Swedish Death Cleaning Quotes* https://www.goodreads.com/work/quotes/56664144-d-st-dning-ingen-sorglig-historia
- *Mental Health Benefits of Decluttering* https://www.webmd.com/mental-health/mental-health-benefits-of-decluttering
- *LEGACY PLANNING WORKSHEET* https://sp-comm-arkfiles.s3.theark.cloud/website/pdfs/Legacy_Giving/Legacy%20Planning%20Worksheet.pdf
- *6 Swedish Death Cleaning Strategies to Free You from ...* https://www.bhg.com/decorating/storage/organization-basics/swedish-death-cleaning-tips/
- *The Many Mental Benefits of Decluttering* https://www.psychologytoday.com/us/blog/the-resilient-brain/202302/the-many-mental-benefits-of-decluttering
- *Fika like a Swede – what Swedish fika is and 5 classic ...* https://visitsweden.com/what-to-do/food-drink/swedish-kitchen/all-about-swedish-fika/
- *The Ultimate Decluttering Checklist to Get You Started* https://www.happysimplemom.com/decluttering-checklist/
- *What is Swedish death cleaning and how can it benefit you?* https://patient.info/news-and-features/what-is-swedish-death-cleaning-and-how-can-it-benefit-you
- *The KonMari Approach to Sentimental Items* https://konmari.com/how-to-konmari-sentimental-objects/?srsltid=AfmBOooJmnoRaAIHCcFvosESQqShX3F9zkrejlTlKh17UJRBSId65AB6
- *35 Journal Prompts for Decluttering Your Home and Life* https://balancethroughsimplicity.com/journal-prompts-for-decluttering/
- *I Tried Swedish Death Cleaning (And It Changed How I ...* https://www.goodhousekeeping.com/home/cleaning/a63299997/i-tried-swedish-death-cleaning/

BIBLIOGRAPHY

- *Swedish Death Cleaning Is the Secret to an Organized Home* https://www.marthastewart.com/swedish-death-cleaning-8716891
- *Decluttering the Nest Can Help You Move Forward* https://sixtyandme.com/decluttering-the-nest-helping-your-adult-children-and-you-to-move-forward/
- *How to Stop Arguing About Clutter* https://kathilipp.com/2018/07/how-to-stop-arguing-about-clutter/
- *Swedish Death Cleaning: 5 Reasons to Do It Yourself* https://www.nextavenue.org/swedish-death-cleaning-do-it-yourself/
- *A Simple Step-by-Step Swedish Death Cleaning Checklist* https://tidymalism.com/swedish-death-cleaning-checklist/
- *Why this Scandi philosophy is helping me declutter my home* https://www.livingetc.com/advice/lagom-decluttering
- *Scandinavian Capsule Wardrobe 2025* https://www.lilycherie.com/blog/scandinavian-capsule-wardrobe
- *How to Put Together Your Legacy Drawer* https://www.ramseysolutions.com/retirement/legacy-drawer-keep-your-family-prepared?srsltid=AfmBOopADzjshggESpOqCiFcoGpoYKFGo2NbMO4X9iwyA_dwweuGhM6H
- *6 Steps to Discover the Stories of Your Family Heirlooms* https://familytreemagazine.com/preservation/six-steps-to-heirloom-history/
- *The 4 Best Ways to Digitize Photos (and How to Store Them)* https://shotkit.com/digitize-photos/
- *Digital Legacy Checklist: What to Include in Your Digital Vault* https://mygoodtrust.com/articles/digital-legacy-checklist-what-to-include-in-your-goodtrust-vault
- *A Simple Step-by-Step Swedish Death Cleaning Checklist* https://tidymalism.com/swedish-death-cleaning-checklist/
- *11 Charities That Offer Free Donation Pick Up* https://www.meatheadmovers.com/blog/11-charities-that-offer-free-donation-pick-up/
- *Avoiding Charity Scams* https://www.charitynavigator.org/donor-basics/protect-your-giving/avoid-charity-scams/
- *Ultimate Guide to Recycling Unwanted Items: Eco-Friendly ...* https://www.apexdumpstersinc.com/recycling-unwanted-items
- *Letting Go of Sentimental Items* https://www.theminimalists.com/sentimental/
- *A Simple Step-by-Step Swedish Death Cleaning Checklist* https://tidymalism.com/swedish-death-cleaning-checklist/

BIBLIOGRAPHY

- *8 Best Planners for Decluttering and Maintaining an ...* https://organizeeveryroom.com/best-planners-for-decluttering/
- *Accountability Buddy: How Mutual Responsibility Leads ... - Pact* https://withpact.com/blog/accountability-buddy-how-mutual-responsibility-leads-to-epic-wins
- *Swedish Traditions: Guide to Sweden's Cultural Celebrations* https://www.campervansweden.com/blog/about-sweden/swedish-traditions

www.ingramcontent.com/pod-product-compliance
Lightning Source LLC
Chambersburg PA
CBHW030220100526
44584CB00014BA/1373